Clucks to Chicken: A Beginner's Guide to Raising Chickens and Getting Fresh Eggs Daily from Your Homemade Coop

Unique Kade

Table of Contents

Introduction

Have you ever dreamed of having your flock of chickens and enjoying fresh eggs daily? Do you want a fun and rewarding hobby that benefits your health and the environment? Do you love animals and want to raise them with care and respect?

If you answered yes to these questions, this book is for you!

Raising chickens is not only a great way to produce your food but also an excellent way to enrich your life. Chickens are smart, social, and entertaining creatures who make you smile and laugh with their antics. They will also provide you with nutritious and delicious eggs and meat that you can use in various recipes. By raising your chickens, you will also reduce your environmental impact and support ethical farming practices.

But how do you start raising chickens? What do you need to know and do to keep them happy and healthy? How do you choose the right breed, build a coop, feed and care for them, collect and store eggs, and deal with common problems and challenges?

Don't worry; this book will guide you through every step of the process. You will learn everything you need to know about raising chickens, from choosing the right breed for your needs to building a cozy and safe chicken coop to feeding and caring for your chickens to collecting and storing fresh eggs, raising meat chickens, to hatching and raising baby chicks, to solving common problems and challenges.

This book is written in a **friendly** and **personal** tone, with practical tips and advice, as well as fun facts and anecdotes. You will feel like you have a friend who is an expert on raising chickens by your side.

By the end of this book, you will have all the knowledge and skills you need to raise chickens and enjoy fresh eggs every day. You will also have a lot of fun and satisfaction along the way. You will discover how raising chickens will change your life for the better.

So what are you waiting for? Grab this book and start your chicken adventure today!

Transformative Impacts of Raising Chickens

Raising chickens transcends mere hobby status; it evolves into a lifestyle that ushers in many positive changes. The decision to nurture chickens brings forth a cascade of benefits that fundamentally alter the fabric of your daily existence. Here's an in-depth exploration of how raising chickens will intricately change your life for the better:

1. Daily Bounty of Fresh Eggs:

- ★ Experience the unparalleled joy of indulging in fresh eggs harvested from your flock daily.
- ★ Revel in the superior taste and quality that stems from knowing precisely what your

chickens consume and how they are cared for.

★ Achieve the satisfaction of producing your food while saving money and reducing environmental waste by sidestepping store-bought eggs in plastic cartons.

2. A Gratifying and Enjoyable Hobby:

★ Raising chickens emerges as a source of immeasurable fun and fulfillment.

★ Witness the fascinating journey of your chickens' growth, observing their interactions and distinct personalities.

★ Acquire new skills and knowledge in animal husbandry, biology, and ecology, fostering a sense of accomplishment and pride in providing your chickens with a good life.

3. Health and Environmental Advantages:

★ Elevate your health and contribute to a healthier environment by raising chickens.

★ Immerse yourself in outdoor activities with your chickens, promoting increased exercise and exposure to fresh air.

★ Alleviate stress and anxiety by engaging with your chickens and relishing the soothing sounds of their presence.

★ Play a role in environmental stewardship by minimizing your carbon footprint, recycling kitchen scraps, and producing natural fertilizer for your garden.

4. Community Connection with Fellow Enthusiasts:

★ Raising chickens becomes a bridge to a community of like-minded individuals who share your passion.

★ Engage in exchanging tips, advice, and anecdotes with fellow chicken enthusiasts, building connections, and expanding your social network.

★ Participate in events, activities, and groups centered around chickens, fostering new friendships and a sense of community.

Raising chickens is not just a casual choice; it is a transformative journey that enriches your life in myriad ways. Revel in the daily bounty of fresh eggs, immerse yourself in a gratifying hobby, contribute to your well-being and the environment, and connect with a vibrant community of chicken lovers. Raising chickens is a holistic experience that brings joy, fulfillment, and positive change to every aspect of your life.

Culinary Bliss

Beyond the joy of raising chickens lies the extraordinary delight of savoring fresh eggs and meat from your backyard. This culinary endeavor elevates the taste and unfolds a tapestry of health benefits for you and your family. Delve into the remarkable advantages of relishing fresh eggs and meat cultivated in your sanctuary:

1. Nutrient-Rich Goodness:

- ★ Reap the rewards of higher levels of protein, omega-3 fatty acids, vitamins, and minerals in fresh eggs and meat from your chickens.
- ★ Embrace your chickens' natural and varied diet, free from the additives, hormones,

and antibiotics often found in store-bought counterparts.

2. A Symphony of Flavors:

★ Embark on a culinary journey where fresh eggs and meat tantalize your taste buds with richer flavors, textures, and colors.

★ Appreciate the nuanced taste that sets your homegrown delicacies apart, making every bite a delectable experience.

3. Satiety and Satisfaction:

★ Relish the satisfaction of being filled up and energized for longer durations after consuming fresh eggs and meat.

★ Revel in the balanced and complete meal your homegrown produce provides, enhancing your overall sense of fulfillment.

The benefits of indulging in fresh eggs and meat from your chickens extend beyond taste. Immerse yourself in more nutritious, delicious, and satisfying culinary experiences that improve your physical health and invigorate your palate. Every meal celebrates the remarkable journey from coop to the table, enhancing your appreciation for the culinary delights from your dedication to raising chickens.

Discovering Bliss and Fulfillment Through a Fulfilling Pastime

Are you currently relishing the joy and fulfillment that a beloved hobby can bring into your life? If not, you might overlook one of life's most extraordinary treasures. Cultivating a fun and rewarding hobby is not merely an activity; it's a pathway to profound satisfaction and contentment. Here's an exploration of the myriad reasons why adopting a hobby can significantly enhance your happiness and fulfillment:

1. A Purposeful Pursuit:

★ Engaging in a hobby provides a sense of purpose and accomplishment. It's a conscious choice driven by passion and genuine interest, offering a defined goal to pursue and challenges to conquer.

★ Your chosen hobby becomes a canvas for self-expression, allowing you to showcase your talents and skills. The pride and fulfillment derived from completing a project or mastering a skill associated with your hobby are unparalleled.

2. Stress-Free Retreat:

★ Your hobby becomes a sanctuary for relaxation and stress reduction. It's an activity chosen for its sheer enjoyment and pleasure, offering an escape from the demands and pressures of everyday life.

★ Immersing yourself in your hobby provides a therapeutic release for your emotions, channeling them into a positive and creative outlet. The result? A profound sense of calm and rejuvenation after spending dedicated time on your chosen pursuit.

3. An Enriching Journey:

★ A hobby is not just an activity; it's a continuous journey of enrichment and personal growth. It serves as a dynamic platform for learning, exploration, and discovery.

★ Through your hobby, you embark on a quest to uncover new facets of knowledge and open yourself to unexplored possibilities. The journey extends beyond individual pursuits, connecting you with like-minded individuals who share your passion, fostering new friendships, and expanding your social circle.

★ The diversity of experiences and opportunities accompanying your hobby infuse your life with an intriguing tapestry of interest and excitement.

In essence, cultivating a fun and rewarding hobby transcends the notion of mere enjoyment; it becomes a source of profound joy and fulfillment. You gain a sense of purpose, a refuge for relaxation, and a vehicle for continual enrichment. The decision to embrace a hobby is a commitment to a happier and more fulfilled existence as you weave the threads of accomplishment, relaxation, and enrichment into the fabric of your daily life.

Environmental and Ethical reasons

Embarking on the journey of raising your chickens transcends personal benefits; it emerges as a transformative practice that positively influences the environment and upholds ethical standards for animal welfare. Delving into the realms of sustainability and compassion, here's an in-depth exploration of how raising your chickens significantly contributes to environmental and ethical causes:

1. Curbing Carbon Footprint:

★ By raising your chickens, you take a bold step in reducing your carbon footprint. Factory-farmed eggs and meat are notorious contributors to greenhouse gas emissions, water pollution, and land degradation.

★ The decision to rely on your backyard flock minimizes dependence on industrial-scale farming, saving on transportation and packaging costs. Your environmentally conscious choice directly addresses climate change concerns and contributes to the preservation of natural resources.

2. Revolutionizing Waste Management:

★ Embracing personal chicken farming empowers you to revolutionize waste management. Instead of contributing to landfills or incinerators, your kitchen scraps, garden waste, and paper products find purpose as nourishment for your chickens.

★ The cyclical synergy created by feeding your chickens with leftovers, composting chicken manure, and utilizing eggshells as fertilizer or pest-repellent results in a sustainable, circular economy. Through this practice, you actively participate in waste reduction, emphasizing the value of recycling within your own space.

3. Championing Animal Welfare:

★ Raising your chickens is a resounding endorsement of animal welfare and ethical treatment. In contrast to the plight of factory-farmed chickens subjected to overcrowding, mutilation, disease, and abuse, your chickens enjoy a life of respect and compassion.

★ Personal chicken farming provides your flock with essential elements – ample space, fresh air, sunlight, and the freedom to exhibit natural behaviors. Should you slaughter and process your chickens, the emphasis remains on humane and hygienic practices, setting a benchmark for ethical treatment.

Raising your chickens is a powerful agent of change that extends far beyond personal boundaries. It becomes a conscientious choice to combat climate change, promote sustainable waste management, and champion the cause of ethical treatment for animals. Through personal chicken farming, you enhance your immediate surroundings and contribute to a broader movement focused on environmental sustainability and compassionate living.

Chapter 1

How to Pick the Perfect Breed for Your Goals

One of the first and most important decisions you will make when raising chickens is what breed to choose. There are hundreds of breeds of chickens, each with their characteristics, advantages, and disadvantages. Depending on your goals, you should raise chickens for eggs, meat, both, or simply as pets. You may also have preferences for your chickens' appearance, temperament, and hardiness. In this chapter, you will learn how to pick the perfect breed for your goals based on the following criteria:

1. **Egg production:** How many and what color eggs do you want your chickens to lay?

2. **Meat quality:** How much and what kind of meat do you want your chickens to provide?

3. **Temperament:** How friendly, calm, and docile do you want your chickens to be?

4. **Appearance:** How do you want your chickens to look in size, shape, color, and feather pattern?

5. **Hardiness:** How well do you want your chickens to adapt to different climates, seasons, and environments?

By the end of this chapter, you will have a clear idea of what breed of chickens suits your needs and preferences best. You will also know where and how to find and buy healthy chicks or adult birds from reliable sources. You will be ready to start your chicken adventure with the perfect breed for your goals.

Types and Uniqueness

Chickens come in a remarkable array of breeds, each with distinct features. Here, we'll delve into the characteristics that set various breeds apart.

1. The Heritage Breeds

They include: Rhode Island Reds and Plymouth Rocks, boast a rich history, and are known for their hardiness and traditional qualities.

2. The Egg Layers

Breeds like Leghorns and Sussex are renowned for their exceptional egg-laying capabilities, making them ideal choices for those seeking a steady supply of fresh eggs.

3. The Dual-Purpose Breeds

Dual-purpose breeds like Orpingtons and Australorps are prized for their egg production and meat quality, offering versatility for backyard enthusiasts.

4. The Fancy Breeds

Fancy or ornamental breeds, such as Silkies and Polish, captivate with their unique appearance, adding charm to any flock.

5. The Bantams

Bantam breeds, miniature versions of their larger counterparts, are perfect for smaller spaces and are often kept for their friendly demeanor and decorative appeal.

Rhode Island Reds: The All-American Poultry Powerhouse

Rhode Island Reds (RIR) stand out as one of the most iconic and popular chicken breeds, known for their robust qualities and excellence. Originating in the United States, these birds have become a staple in backyard flocks and commercial operations. Let's explore the unique characteristics that make Rhode Island Reds a favorite among poultry enthusiasts.

1. Heritage and History:

Rhode Island Reds have a rich heritage that dates back to the mid-19th century. Developed in Rhode Island and Massachusetts, these chickens were bred for their exceptional egg-laying abilities and hardiness. Their heritage status means they carry a piece of American agricultural history, making them a cherished part of any flock.

2. Exceptional Egg Production:

One of the standout features of Rhode Island Reds is their remarkable egg-laying prowess. Hens consistently produce large brown eggs, making them an excellent choice for those seeking a regular and abundant supply of fresh eggs. Their reliable performance has earned them a spot among the preferred breeds for egg production.

3. Hardy and Adaptable:

Rhode Island Reds are known for their resilience and adaptability to various climates. These chickens maintain their productivity in summer's scorching heat or winter's chilly temperatures. Their hardiness makes them ideal for backyard enthusiasts and small-scale farmers, requiring less intensive care than more delicate breeds.

4. Dual-Purpose Excellence:

While renowned for their egg-laying capabilities, Rhode Island Reds are also recognized as dual-purpose birds. This means they excel in egg production and as a quality meat source. Their well-developed bodies and fine-textured meat make them a practical choice for raising chickens for both eggs and meat.

5. Friendly Disposition:

Beyond their practical attributes, Rhode Island Reds are known for their friendly and docile nature. They often establish a strong connection with their human caretakers, making them an excellent choice for families with children or those seeking a more interactive chicken-keeping experience. Their affable demeanor adds a delightful aspect to the overall chicken-raising journey.

6. Distinctive Appearance:

Rhode Island Reds have a classic appearance, with rich, deep red plumage that exudes a warm and inviting charm.

Their medium size, single comb, and yellow legs contribute to their traditional and timeless aesthetic. These birds' visual appeal makes them productive and visually pleasing additions to any backyard or farm.

Plymouth Rocks: The Timeless Dual-Purpose Delight

Plymouth Rocks, often called "Rocks," are a classic and enduring breed that has stood the test of time. Known for their dual-purpose qualities, friendly temperament, and striking appearance, Plymouth Rocks have become a staple in backyard flocks and small-scale farming operations. Let's delve into the unique characteristics that make Plymouth Rocks a standout choice for poultry enthusiasts.

1. Historical Heritage:

Plymouth Rocks have a storied history, with roots tracing back to the mid-19th century in the United States. Developed in Massachusetts, these chickens quickly gained popularity for their versatility and adaptability.

The breed played a significant role in developing modern poultry farming, contributing to the success of small-scale and backyard chicken keeping.

2. Dual-Purpose Excellence:

One of the defining features of Plymouth Rocks is their exceptional dual-purpose nature. These birds are proficient in egg production and meat quality, making them a well-rounded choice for those seeking versatility in their flock. The hens reliably lay large brown eggs, while the roosters boast a plump and flavorful carcass, making them suitable for home egg production and meat consumption.

3. Cold-Hardy and Adaptable:

Plymouth Rocks are renowned for their hardiness and adaptability to various climates. Their thick and downy feathers provide insulation, making them well-suited for colder regions. This adaptability and easygoing nature make them an excellent choice for novice chicken keepers and those living in diverse environmental conditions.

4. Docile Temperament:

Plymouth Rocks are known for their calm and friendly demeanor, making them an ideal addition to family flocks. Their gentle nature makes them easy to handle, and they tend to get along well with other chickens, promoting a harmonious environment in the coop. This friendly disposition also makes them suitable for educational purposes and interaction with children.

5. Distinctive Appearance:

The Plymouth Rock's appearance is distinctive and eye-catching. The Barred Plymouth Rock is the most common variety with its black and white striped plumage.

This classic barred pattern gives them a timeless and elegant look that adds a touch of charm to any flock. Other varieties, such as the White Plymouth Rock, also exhibit appealing coloration that contributes to their overall visual appeal.

6. Ease of Care:

Plymouth Rocks is known for its low maintenance care requirements. Their robust health, resistance to common poultry ailments, and ability to forage for food make them a practical choice for experienced and novice chicken keepers. Their self-sufficiency and dual-purpose qualities make them an economical and rewarding addition to any backyard or small farm.

Sussex Chickens: A Multifaceted Marvel in the Poultry World

Sussex chickens stand as a testament to the diversity and versatility within the poultry world.

Known for their exceptional qualities in various aspects, Sussex chickens have captured the hearts of backyard enthusiasts and commercial farmers alike. Let's delve into the extensive features that make Sussex chickens unique and cherished in the poultry community.

1. Heritage and History:

The Sussex breed has a rich history dating back to the early 20th century in England. These chickens were initially developed in Sussex County, and their enduring popularity can be attributed to their adaptive nature and excellent production qualities. Sussex chickens quickly gained recognition for their utility, charm, and ease of care.

2. Remarkable Egg Production:

Sussex chickens are revered for their consistent and impressive egg-laying abilities. Hens of the Sussex breed reliably produce a substantial number of large brown eggs, making them an excellent choice for those seeking a regular supply of fresh eggs.

This reliable performance has contributed to Sussex chickens being considered among the top breeds for egg production.

3. Dual-Purpose Excellence:

Beyond their prowess in egg production, Sussex chickens are celebrated as dual-purpose birds. They exhibit a well-balanced build, with plump bodies suitable for meat production. Their efficient egg-laying capabilities and quality meat production make Sussex chickens a versatile choice for small-scale farmers and backyard keepers.

4. Varied Color Varieties:

One of the striking features of Sussex chickens is the wide array of color varieties they come in. From the classic Sussex with white feathers and black markings to the Speckled Sussex with its distinctive speckled plumage and variations such as Red, Buff, and Silver Sussex, each variety adds a vibrant and visually appealing touch to any flock.

5. Docile Temperament:

Sussex chickens are known for their docile and friendly nature. Their calm disposition makes them a delight to work with, especially for families and those looking for chickens with gentle temperaments. This generous nature enhances the overall enjoyment of chicken keeping and makes Sussex chickens suitable for interaction with children.

6. Adaptability to Various Climates:

Sussex chickens exhibit remarkable adaptability to different climates, making them suitable for various geographical locations. Sussex chickens maintain their health and productivity, whether in the heat of summer or winter cold. This adaptability contributes to their popularity among chicken keepers in diverse regions.

7. Resistance to Common Ailments:

Sussex chickens are known for their robust health and resistance to common poultry ailments. Their hardiness reduces the likelihood of diseases, making them a practical choice for those prioritizing low-maintenance care and a reduced need for medical interventions.

8. Heritage and Exhibition Qualities:

Beyond their practical utility, certain Sussex varieties, such as the Speckled Sussex, have gained popularity in poultry exhibitions. The distinctive and attractive plumage of Sussex chickens adds to their appeal, making them a favorite choice for those interested in participating in poultry shows.

<u>Leghorns: The Pinnacle of Egg-Laying Prowess and Adaptability</u>

Leghorns, often called the "queens of egg production," are a standout breed in the poultry world. Known for their unparalleled laying abilities, Leghorns have earned a reputation as efficient and prolific egg producers. Let's explore the extensive qualities that make Leghorns unique and cherished in chicken keeping.

1. Heritage and History:

Leghorns have a rich heritage that traces back to Italy, where they were initially developed. The breed made its way to the United States in the early 1800s and quickly gained popularity for its exceptional egg-laying capabilities. Leghorns were pivotal in shaping the commercial egg industry and remain a cornerstone in backyard flocks today.

2. Unrivaled Egg Production:

The standout feature of Leghorns lies in their unmatched egg-laying prowess. Leghorn hens are known to lay large, white eggs consistently and prolifically. Their ability to lay upwards of 280 to 320 eggs per year makes them the breed of choice for those primarily focused on egg production, whether for personal consumption or commercial purposes.

3. Efficient Feed Conversion:

Leghorns are highly efficient in converting feed into eggs. Their slender and athletic build allows them to channel their energy primarily into egg production rather than body mass. This efficiency contributes to their prolific laying and makes them a cost-effective choice for those mindful of feed expenses.

4. Active and Foraging Nature:

Leghorns are known for their active and foraging behavior. These energetic birds are excellent foragers, scratching the ground for insects and plants. Their natural foraging instincts contribute to a diet supplemented with various nutrients, making them well-suited for free-range or pasture-based systems.

5. Adaptability to Various Climates:

Leghorns are highly adaptable to different climates, making them suitable for various geographical locations. Their ability to thrive in hot and cold environments further enhances their versatility and popularity among chicken keepers worldwide.

6. Distinctive Appearance:

Leghorns exhibit a distinctive appearance characterized by their sleek and elegant build. They have a single comb, white earlobes, and bright red wattles. The classic white variety is the most common. Still, other types, such as Brown Leghorns, add a touch of diversity to their visual appeal.

7. Flighty and Independent Temperament:
Leghorns are known for their more flighty and independent temperament than other breeds. While they may be less inclined to seek human interaction, their active nature and independence make them well-suited for free-range environments and less dependent on constant human attention.

8. Commercial Significance:
Leghorns have significant commercial importance, particularly in the egg industry. Large-scale egg production operations often favor Leghorns due to their prolific laying and efficient feed conversion. The breed's contribution to the commercial egg sector has

solidified its status as a cornerstone in the global poultry industry.

Australorps: The Australian Giants of Productivity and Gentleness

Australorps, short for Australian Orpingtons, have carved a special niche in the poultry world, celebrated for their outstanding egg-laying capabilities, friendly demeanor, and attractive appearance. Let's delve into the extensive qualities that make Australorps a fascinating and cherished chicken-keeping breed.

1. Historical Roots:

Australorps originated in Australia in the early 20th century. The breed was developed by crossing Black Orpingtons with Rhode Island Reds and White Leghorns, aiming to create a chicken with superior egg-laying abilities. The result was Australorps, which quickly gained recognition for breaking world records in egg production.

2. Exceptional Egg Production:

Australorps are renowned for their exceptional egg-laying prowess. These chickens consistently produce large brown eggs, and the breed holds the world record for the most eggs laid in a year by a single hen. The commitment to egg production makes Australorps an excellent choice for those prioritizing a steady supply of fresh eggs.

3. Dual-Purpose Qualities:

While Australorps are primarily celebrated for their egg-laying abilities, they are also considered dual-purpose birds. Their well-rounded build and meat quality make them suitable for egg and meat production. This versatility adds to their appeal for those looking to raise chickens, contributing to various aspects of a self-sustaining flock.

4. Gentle and Docile Temperament:

Australorps are known for their gentle and docile nature. Their calm demeanor and friendly disposition make them an ideal choice for families, as they are often more tolerant of handling and human interaction. This amiable temperament enhances the overall experience of raising Australorps and contributes to their popularity among backyard enthusiasts.

5. Black Beauty:

The Australorp's striking appearance adds to its allure. The breed is typically black with a vibrant green sheen to its feathers. This glossy and lustrous plumage gives Australorps a distinctive and beautiful aesthetic that stands out in any flock.

6. Adaptability and Hardiness:

Australorps exhibit adaptability and hardiness, making them well-suited for various climates. Their ability to thrive in different environmental conditions contributes to their versatility, allowing chicken keepers in various regions to enjoy the benefits of Australorp ownership.

7. Efficient Feed Conversion:

Australorps are known for their efficient feed conversion. While they may not be as slender as some egg-focused breeds, their ability to turn feed into eggs and meat is commendable. This efficiency is particularly advantageous for those seeking a practical and sustainable flock.

8. Heritage and Recognition:

Australorps carry a legacy of excellence, having gained international recognition for their egg-laying achievements. The breed has not only held world records but has also become a symbol of Australian poultry pride. This heritage adds a layer of significance to the breed and underscores its importance in the history of poultry keeping.

Orpingtons: The Majestic and Gentle Giants of the Poultry World

Orpingtons, often called the "gentle giants" of the chicken world, are a beloved and iconic breed known for their regal appearance, dual-purpose qualities, and calm temperament. Let's delve into the extensive characteristics that make Orpingtons a cherished and popular choice among chicken enthusiasts.

1. Historical Heritage:

Orpingtons originated in England in the late 1800s, developed by William Cook in Orpington. The breed was created by crossing various breeds, including Langshans, Minorcas, and Plymouth Rocks, to achieve a large, dual-purpose bird with a friendly disposition. Orpingtons quickly gained popularity and became one of the most sought-after breeds during the early 20th century.

2. Majestic Appearance:

Orpingtons are known for their majestic and imposing appearance. These birds have a large, broad, and well-feathered body, giving them a substantial and regal presence. They come in various color varieties, including Black, Blue, Buff, and White, each with unique and attractive plumage.

3. Dual-Purpose Excellence:

Orpingtons are celebrated as dual-purpose birds, excelling in egg production and meat quality. Their large size contributes to substantial meat yields, and hens are reliable layers of large brown eggs. This dual-purpose quality makes

Orpingtons a practical choice for raising chickens for sustenance and pleasure.

4. Docile and Friendly Temperament:

Orpingtons are renowned for their docile and friendly temperament. Their calm and easygoing nature makes them an ideal choice for families, as they are often more tolerant of handling and human interaction. Orpingtons' gentle demeanor enhances the overall chicken-keeping experience. It makes them suitable for both novice and experienced poultry enthusiasts.

5. Broodiness and Motherly Instincts:

Orpington hens are known for their strong broody instincts and excellent mothering abilities. They often make exceptional mothers, diligently caring for and protecting their chicks. This characteristic can be advantageous for those interested in the natural hatching and raising of chicks within the flock.

6. Cold-Hardy and Adaptable:

Orpingtons are well-suited to various climates, exhibiting resilience in hot and cold weather. Their thick feathering provides insulation, making them particularly cold-hardy. This adaptability ensures that Orpingtons can thrive in diverse environments, contributing to their popularity among chicken keepers worldwide.

7. Exhibition and Show Qualities:

Certain varieties of Orpingtons, such as the Buff Orpington, have gained recognition in poultry exhibitions and shows. The breed's distinctive appearance and well-defined color patterns appeal to those interested in showcasing their birds and participating in competitive events.

8. Sustainable Foraging Abilities:

While Orpingtons are larger birds, they maintain a balanced and sustainable foraging behavior. Their ability to graze and forage for insects and plants contributes to a well-rounded diet, promoting overall health and minimizing the need for supplemental feed.

9. Heritage and Enduring Popularity:

Orpingtons have retained their popularity over the decades and are considered heritage breeds. Their enduring appeal can be attributed to their practicality, beauty, and amiable temperament. The breed's historic significance adds a layer of cultural and agricultural heritage to Orpington ownership.

Silkies: The Enchanting Fluff Balls of Poultry Elegance

With their distinctive appearance and unique characteristics, Silkies stand out as one of the most enchanting and beloved breeds in the poultry world. Often described as **"fluffy clouds"** or **"feathered teddy bears,"** Silkies captivate chicken enthusiasts with their soft, silk-like plumage and gentle demeanor. Let's delve into the extensive and unique qualities that make Silkies an extraordinary addition to any flock.

1. Ancient Origins and Mystique:

Silkies have ancient origins; their roots can be traced back to China over 2,000 years ago. The breed's arrival in the Western world is shrouded in mystery and tales of exotic allure, adding to their enigmatic charm. Silkies were initially brought to Europe by Marco Polo, and their distinct features have captivated chicken keepers ever since.

2. Soft and Silky Plumage:

The most defining characteristic of Silkies is their soft, silky plumage. Unlike traditional feathers found in other breeds, Silkies have feathers lacking the barbicels that interlock, giving them a fur-like appearance. Combined with their downy under-features, this unique feature creates an irresistibly smooth and fluffy texture.

3. Distinctive Appearance:

Silkies are visually distinct, featuring a combination of unique traits. Their dark blue skin, bearded faces, and five toes (instead of the usual four) set them apart. Their small, round bodies are topped with a crest of feathers resembling a pom-pom, contributing to their whimsical and adorable appearance.

4. Variety in Color:

Silkies come in various colors: white, black, blue, splash, buff, and partridge. Each color variation adds to the breed's allure, providing chicken keepers with options to suit their aesthetic preferences. The diversity in color allows for a visually striking and vibrant flock.

5. Gentle and Calm Temperament:

Silkies are renowned for their gentle and calm temperament. Their easygoing nature makes them excellent companions suitable for families, children, and pets. Silkies are known to be docile and enjoy human interaction, often willingly perching on their caretakers' shoulders.

6. Broodiness and Exceptional Mothering Instincts:

Silkies are considered one of the best broody hens among chicken breeds. Their strong maternal instincts and willingness to sit on eggs make them excellent natural hatchers. Silkies are known to adopt chicks from other hens, showcasing their nurturing and protective qualities.

7. Quirky Behavior and Social Structure:

Silkies exhibit quirky behavior that adds to their charm. Their unique appearance and gentle nature often result in Silkies being accepted into flocks without much conflict. They tend to form close-knit social groups within the flock, contributing to a harmonious and peaceful environment.

8. Popular in Poultry Shows:

Silkies are popular for poultry shows and exhibitions due to their unique appearance and charming demeanor. Their striking features make them stand out in competitions, where they often garner attention and admiration from judges and spectators alike.

9. Indoor Pet Potential:

Due to their calm temperament and small size, Silkies have gained popularity as indoor pets. Some chicken enthusiasts keep Silkies as house pets, allowing them to roam freely in homes or even participate in chicken diaper-wearing activities, showcasing the adaptability of these charming birds.

10.Symbolic and Cultural Significance:

In various cultures, Silkies are associated with different symbolic meanings. In Chinese folklore, Silkies are believed to possess mystical powers and are related to good fortune. In Western cultures, they are often seen as symbols of charm and beauty.

Bantams: Petite Marvels of Poultry Charm and Versatility

Bantams, often described as the "miniature jewels" of the poultry world, are enchanting and endearing small-sized chickens that punch personality and charm. While small, these diminutive birds offer unique characteristics and are celebrated for their versatility, ornamental appeal, and delightful disposition.

1. Miniature Marvels with Historical Roots:

Bantams have a rich history that dates back to the Far East and Southeast Asia. Originally discovered in the jungles of Java, these miniatures were brought to Europe by seafarers and traders in the 15th century. Their tiny size captured the fascination of poultry enthusiasts, leading to the development and widespread popularity of various Bantam breeds.

2. Ornamental Variety and Unique Breeds:

One of the most captivating aspects of Bantam is the vast array of ornamental varieties and unique breeds available. From the delicate and dainty Sebrights to the feathery-footed Cochins and the flamboyant Polish Bantams with their impressive crests, each breed contributes to the ornamental allure of Bantam keeping. Their miniature size allows for an exquisite display of diverse plumage patterns, colors, and feather types.

3. Space-Efficient Poultry Keeping:

Bantams are a practical choice for those with limited space. Their size makes them suitable for urban settings, backyard gardens, and small homesteads where traditional-sized chickens need to be more practical. Bantams provide the opportunity to experience the joys of poultry keeping without the space requirements associated with larger breeds.

4. Dual-Purpose Capabilities:

While Bantams are often admired for their ornamental qualities, many breeds exhibit dual-purpose capabilities. Some Bantams, such as the Old English Game Bantams, have a historical background in cockfighting but are now appreciated for their striking appearance and friendly temperament. Other Bantam breeds, like the Belgian d'Uccle, offer a balance of egg production and ornamental appeal.

5. Friendly and Tame Nature:

Bantams are known for their friendly and tame nature. Their small size and gentle disposition make them approachable and suitable for families with children. Bantams often enjoy interaction with their caretakers, fostering a close bond that adds to the joy of keeping these petite poultry companions.

6. Broodiness and Exceptional Mothering Instincts:

Bantam hens are renowned for their strong broodiness and exceptional mothering instincts. Despite their small size, many Bantam breeds excel as nurturing mothers, diligently caring for their chicks. Their protective and devoted behavior enhances the experience of natural hatching and rearing within the flock.

7. Entertaining and Energetic Behavior: Bantams are known for their entertaining and energetic behavior. Their small size allows for agility and lively movement, making them a joy to watch. Bantams often engage in dust bathing, foraging, and playful interactions with their flock mates, adding a dynamic and animated element to poultry keeping.

8. Showmanship and Exhibition: Bantams are popular choices for poultry shows and exhibitions. Many Bantam breeds' ornamental nature and unique characteristics often make them stand out in competitive events. Breeders and enthusiasts appreciate the challenge of perfecting the miniature standards set for the Bantam exhibition.

9. Collectors' Favorites:

Bantams are often favored by collectors and enthusiasts who appreciate the diversity of colors, patterns, and feather types within the Bantam world. The pursuit of collecting and breeding unique Bantam varieties becomes a hobby in itself, with individuals drawn to the challenge of maintaining and improving specific traits within these miniature marvels.

Polish Chickens: The Glamorous Aristocrats of the Poultry Runway

With their striking appearance and distinctive crests, Polish chickens stand out as the glamorous aristocrats of the poultry world. Known for their elegant plumage and captivating headgear, Polish chickens are a favorite among poultry enthusiasts and exhibition breeders. Let's delve into the extensive and unique qualities that make Polish chickens a delightful and visually arresting addition to any flock.

1. Historical Heritage and European Roots:

Polish chickens have a rich history that traces back to their European origins, possibly Poland or the Netherlands. They were introduced to Western Europe in the 16th century and quickly gained popularity for their ornamental qualities. The breed's charming appearance and unique crests have made them a symbol of elegance and style.

2. Striking Headgear:

The most iconic feature of Polish chickens is their elaborate crest of feathers that adorn their heads. This distinctive headgear, resembling a stylish hat, comes in various styles, including the V-shaped crest, the bouffant crest, and the globular crest. The crests can be adorned with feathers that match the bird's body color, creating a visually captivating and regal appearance.

3. Ornamental Variety and Colors:

Polish chickens come in various colors, adding to their ornamental appeal. Each color variation contributes to the breed's aesthetic diversity, from the classic White Crested Black Polish to the Silver Laced Polish and the Buff Laced Polish. The colorful plumage and unique head crest make Polish chickens stand out in any flock.

4. Good Egg Layers with a Twist:

While Polish chickens are primarily kept for ornamental purposes and exhibition, they are also known to be good egg layers. Hens lay a respectable number of medium-sized white eggs. However, their distinctive crests can pose challenges, as the feathers may obstruct their vision, making them more susceptible to predation and environmental hazards.

5. Friendly and Docile Temperament:
Despite their regal appearance, Polish chickens are known for their friendly and docile temperament. They are often amiable and enjoy human interaction, making them suitable for families and individuals seeking chickens with a gentle disposition. Their calm nature adds to the overall enjoyment of keeping these elegant birds.

6. Challenges with Crest Maintenance:
While stunning, the impressive crests of Polish chickens require some extra care. Owners must be attentive to the crests, ensuring they remain clean and debris-free. Trimming may be necessary to prevent the feathers from obstructing the bird's vision, and some enthusiasts even fashion tiny hairnets to protect the crest.

7. Unique Waddle and Comb:

In addition to their extraordinary crests, Polish chickens have a distinct V-shaped comb and a unique, pendant-style waddle. These features contribute to their overall elegance and complete the aristocratic look that defines the breed.

8. Popular in Poultry Shows:

Polish chickens are highly popular in poultry shows and exhibitions. Their unique appearance, diverse colors, and regal demeanor make them stand out on the exhibition floor. Breeders and enthusiasts often showcase their Polish chickens, competing for recognition and awards in various categories.

9. Backyard Ornamental Favorites:

While Polish chickens may have originated as aristocrats of the European countryside, they have become favorites in backyard flocks for their ornamental charm. Their graceful presence adds a touch of glamor to any flock, making them a sought-after choice for those looking to elevate the visual appeal of their poultry.

Conclusion

In conclusion, each chicken breed discussed contributes uniquely to poultry keeping:

- **Leghorns:** Prolific egg layers with unmatched adaptability.
- **Sussex:** A harmonious blend of history, utility, and charm with exceptional egg production.
- **Plymouth Rocks:** Celebrated for historical significance and dual-purpose excellence.
- **Rhode Island Reds:** Well-rounded and adaptable, with exceptional egg production.

- **Australorps:** Giants of productivity and gentleness with historical roots and adaptability.

- **Orpingtons:** Majestic and gentle giants, known for a regal appearance and enduring popularity.

- **Silkies:** Enchant with soft plumage, a unique appearance, and cultural significance.

- **Polish Chickens:** Glamorous aristocrats with historical heritage, striking headgear, and ornamental variety.

- **Bantams:** Miniature marvels, offering enchantment with ornamental variety, space efficiency, and showmanship appeal.

Each breed provides a distinct and rewarding experience, catering to the preferences and goals of poultry enthusiasts worldwide.

Matching Each Breed to Your Needs and Preference

When you choose a chicken breed, you will want to consider four main factors: egg production, meat quality, temperament, and appearance. These factors determine how well your chickens will suit your goals and expectations. Here is how to match these factors to your needs and preferences:

1. Egg production:

This factor refers to how many eggs your chickens will lay and what color they will be. Some breeds are more prolific than others, and some lay different colored eggs, such as white, brown, blue, or green. You must choose a breed according to how many eggs you want and what color you prefer. For example, if you want a lot of eggs, you may select an ISA Brown, which can lay up to 300 or more eggs a year. If you wish to have blue eggs, you may choose an Araucana, which lays beautiful blue eggs.

2. Meat quality:

This factor refers to how much and what kind of meat your chickens will provide. Some breeds are more suitable for meat production than others, and some have different meat characteristics, such as flavor, texture, and tenderness. You must choose a breed according to how much and what kind of meat you want. For example, if you want a lot of meat, you may select a Cornish Cross, which can grow up to 10 pounds in 8 weeks. You may choose a Barred Plymouth Rock with rich and tender meat if you want more flavorful meat.

3. Temperament:

This factor refers to how friendly, calm, and docile your chickens will be. Some breeds are more sociable and easy-going than others, and some are more nervous and flighty. Depending on how you want to interact with your chickens and how well they will get along with each other and other animals, you must choose a breed accordingly. For example, suppose you want a friendly and cuddly chicken. In that case, you may choose a Silkie, which is very sweet and affectionate. If you want a calm and mellow chicken, you may choose a Barred Plymouth Rock, which is very laid-back and gentle.

4. Appearance:

This factor refers to how your chickens look in size, shape, color, and feather pattern. Some breeds are more attractive and distinctive than others, and some have special features, such as crests, beards, or feathered feet. You must choose a breed according to how you want your chickens to look and how much you care about their appearance.

For example, suppose you want a beautiful and elegant chicken. In that case, you may choose an Andalusian with a slender, graceful body with blue feathers. If you want a unique and quirky chicken, you may choose a Turken with a naked neck that makes it look like it is missing feathers.

By matching these factors to your needs and preferences, you can pick the perfect breed for your goals. You will also be able to enjoy the diversity and variety of chickens and appreciate their different qualities and personalities.

How to find and buy healthy chicks or adult birds from reputable sources

Once you have decided on a breed of chickens, you must find and buy healthy chicks or adult birds from reputable sources. This is a crucial step, as it will affect the health and happiness of your chickens and the success of your chicken adventure. Here are some tips on how to find and buy healthy chicks or adult birds from reputable sources:

1. Do your research:

Before buying any chicks or adult birds, you will need to research the source. You will want to find out where they come from, how they are raised, what they are fed, and how they are treated.

You will also want to check their reputation, reviews, and references. You will want to avoid unlicensed, unprofessional, or unethical sources, as they may sell you sick, injured, mistreated chickens, or even scam you.

2. Choose your source:

There are different sources where you can buy chicks or adult birds, such as hatcheries, breeders, feed stores, farmers, or online platforms. Each source has pros and cons, and you must choose the one that best suits your needs and preferences.

For example, if you want a large selection of breeds, you may select a hatchery that can mail you chicks. If you want a more personal and local service, choose a breeder who can let you visit their farm and see their chickens. If you want a more convenient and affordable option, choose a feed store that can sell you chicks or adult birds in person.

If you want a more flexible and diverse option, choose an online platform like Craigslist or Facebook, which can connect you with other chicken owners selling or giving away their chickens.

3. Inspect your chickens:

Before you buy any chicks or adult birds, you will need to scrutinize them for any signs of illness, injury, or stress. You will want to look at their eyes, ears, nose, mouth, feathers, skin, legs, feet, and vent. You will want to avoid chickens with any symptoms: discharge, swelling, bleeding, scabs, lice, mites, worms, diarrhea, lameness, deformity, or abnormal behavior. You will also want to check their gender, age, and breed and ensure they match what you want and are paying for.

4. Transport your chickens:

After buying your chicks or adult birds, you must transport them safely and comfortably to your home.

Things you will need include:

- A suitable container, such as a cardboard box, a plastic crate, or a wire cage, that is well-ventilated, secure, and spacious.

- Bedding that is clean, dry, and absorbent, such as straw, shavings, or paper towels.

- Provision of water, food, and heat, depending on the distance and duration of the transport.

- Avoiding exposing your chickens to extreme temperatures, loud noises, or rough handling, as they may cause stress or harm.

Following these tips, you can find and buy healthy chicks or adult birds from reputable sources. You can also start your chicken adventure with confidence and excitement.

How to prevent and treat common chicken diseases and keep your flock healthy

Keeping your chickens healthy is one of the most critical and challenging aspects of raising chickens. Chickens are susceptible to various diseases and parasites, affecting their productivity, quality, and longevity. Some of these diseases and parasites can also be transmitted to humans and other animals, posing a risk to your health and safety. Therefore, you must prevent and treat common chicken diseases and keep your flock healthy. Here are some ways to do that:

1. Prevent diseases:

Prevention is better than cure, and the best way to prevent diseases is to provide your chickens with a clean, comfortable, and safe environment. **You will need to:**

- Keep your coop run clean and dry and remove any feces, bedding, feed, or water that is dirty or spoiled.

- Provide your chickens with fresh water, nutritious food, and adequate space and protect them from predators, pests, and weather.

- Quarantine new or sick chickens and avoid introducing foreign objects, animals, or people that may carry diseases or parasites.

2. Treat diseases:

Despite your best efforts, your chickens may still get sick or infected by diseases or parasites. In that case, you must treat them as soon as possible and prevent spreading the disease or parasite to the rest of the flock.

You must:

- Identify the disease or parasite and use the appropriate medication, treatment, or remedy.

- Isolate the sick or infected chickens, disinfect the coop and run, and any equipment or tools that may be contaminated.

- Consult a veterinarian if the disease or parasite is serious, unfamiliar, or unresponsive to treatment.

3. **Monitor your chickens:**

The key to preventing and treating diseases is to monitor your chickens regularly and closely and look for any signs or symptoms of illness or infection. You must observe your chickens' behavior, appearance, and output and check for changes or abnormalities. You must also perform routine health checks and examine your chickens' eyes, ears, nose, mouth, feathers, skin, legs, feet, and vents. You must also keep records of your chickens' health and note any issues or treatments.

You can keep your flock healthy and happy by preventing and treating common chicken diseases. You will also enjoy the benefits of raising chickens and avoiding risks or losses.

Chapter 2

How to Build a Comfortable and Secure Chicken Coop

After you have chosen your chicken breed, you will need to build a comfortable and secure chicken coop for them. A chicken coop is more than just a shelter; it is a home for your chickens. It will provide them with protection, comfort, and happiness. It will also make your chicken adventure easier and more enjoyable. In this chapter, you will learn how to build a comfortable and secure chicken coop based on the following requirements:

- The essential requirements for a chicken coop that will keep your chickens happy and safe

- How to choose the best location, size, ventilation, insulation, and flooring for your coop

- How to provide nesting boxes, roosts, feeders, and waterers for your chickens

- How to protect your chickens from predators and intruders.

- You will learn how to make your coop predator-proof and secure and deter or deal with unwanted visitors, such as raccoons, foxes, hawks, dogs, or humans.

By the end of this chapter, you will have a clear idea of how to build a comfortable and secure chicken coop for your chickens. You will be ready to start your coop project and create a cozy and safe home for your chickens.

Requirements

A chicken coop is more than just a shelter; it is a home for your chickens. It will provide them with protection, comfort, and happiness. It will also make your chicken adventure easier and more enjoyable. Therefore, you will need to ensure that your chicken coop meets the essential requirements to keep your chickens happy and safe. These requirements are:

1. **Space:**

Your chickens need space to move around, stretch their wings, and exercise. You must provide at least 4 square feet of floor space per chicken inside the coop and at least 10 square feet of run space per chicken outside the coop. You must also avoid overcrowding, which can cause stress, aggression, and disease among your chickens.

2. **Ventilation:**

Your chickens need fresh air to breathe and regulate their body temperature. You must provide adequate ventilation in your coop by installing windows, vents, or fans. You will also need to ensure that the ventilation is clear, as it can cause your chickens to be cold, damp, and have respiratory problems.

3. **Insulation:**

Your chickens must stay warm in the winter and cool in the summer. You will need to insulate your coop by using materials such as wood, straw, or foam. You must also avoid overheating, as it can cause heat stress, dehydration, and reduced egg production for your chickens.

4. **Flooring:**

Your chickens will need a clean and dry floor to walk on and to prevent diseases and parasites. You must choose a suitable flooring material for your coop, such as wood, concrete, or dirt. You must also cover the floor with bedding, such as straw, shavings, or sand, and change it regularly.

5. **Nesting boxes:**

Your chickens need a cozy and private place to lay their eggs. You will need to provide nesting boxes for your chickens using wood, plastic, or metal materials. You must also line the nesting boxes with bedding, such as straw, shavings, or hay, and keep them clean and dry.

6. **Roosts:**

Your chickens will need a comfortable and secure place to sleep at night. You must provide roosts for your chickens using materials such as wood, metal, or PVC. You will also need to place the roosts at least 2 feet above the ground and at least 1 foot apart and ensure they are sturdy and stable.

7. **Feeders and waterers:**

Your chickens will need constant food and water to stay healthy and productive. You must provide feeders and waterers for your chickens using metal, plastic, or ceramic materials. You will also need to place the feeders and waterers in a convenient and accessible location and keep them clean and full.

You can build a comfortable and secure chicken coop for your chickens by meeting these essential requirements. You will also be able to provide them with a happy and safe home.

<u>Location</u>

Choosing the best location for your chicken coop is one of the most important decisions when raising chickens. The location of your coop will affect your chickens' health, happiness, and productivity, as well as your convenience and enjoyment. Therefore, you must consider several factors when choosing the best location for your chicken coop. These factors are:

1. **Sunlight:**

Your chickens need sunlight to regulate their body temperature, stimulate their egg production, and boost their immune system. You must choose a location that receives at least 6 hours of sunlight daily, preferably in the morning and afternoon. You will also need to avoid locations that are too hot or shady, as they can cause heat stress or respiratory problems for your chickens.

2. **Drainage:**

Your chickens will need a dry and clean floor to walk on and to prevent diseases and parasites. You will need to choose a location that has good drainage and that does not collect water or mud. You will also need to keep locations low and too flat, as they can cause flooding or dampness for your chickens.

3. **Wind:**

Your chickens need fresh air to breathe and regulate their body temperature. You will need to choose a location with adequate ventilation that does not block the wind. You will also need to avoid locations that are too windy or too drafty, as they can cause cold, dust, or respiratory problems for your chickens.

4. **Noise:**

Your chickens need a quiet, peaceful environment to sleep and lay eggs. You must choose a location that is away from noise sources, such as traffic, neighbors, or dogs. You will also need to avoid locations too close to your house or your neighbors, as your chickens may make noise that can disturb you or them.

5. **Accessibility:**

You will need convenient and easy access to your chicken coop, as you will need to visit it daily to feed, water, collect eggs, and clean. You must choose a location close to your house, water, and electricity source. You will also need to avoid locations that are too far or difficult to reach, as they can make your chicken adventure more challenging and less enjoyable.

You can choose the best location for your chicken coop by considering these factors. You can also provide your chickens with a comfortable and secure home.

Size

Choosing the best size for your chicken coop is another crucial decision when raising chickens. The size of your coop will affect your chickens' comfort, health, and productivity, as well as your convenience and budget. Therefore, you must consider several factors when choosing the best size for your chicken coop. These factors are:

1. **Number of chickens:**

The number of chickens you plan to have will determine how much space you need to provide them. Generally, you must provide at least 4 square feet of floor space per chicken inside the coop and at least 10 square feet of run space outside the coop. This will ensure your chickens have enough room to move around, stretch their wings, exercise, and avoid overcrowding, stress, aggression, and disease.

2. **Breed of chickens:**

The breed of chickens you have or plan to have will also affect how much space you need to provide them. Different breeds of chickens have different sizes, shapes, and weights; some may need more or less space than others. For example, a bantam chicken, which is a small and lightweight chicken, may need only 2 square feet of floor space per chicken inside the coop and 4 square feet of run space per chicken outside the coop.

On the other hand, a Jersey Giant, which is a large and heavy chicken, may need up to 6 square feet of floor space per chicken inside the coop and 12 square feet of run space per chicken outside the coop.

3. Coop design:

The design of your coop will also affect how much space you will need to provide for your chickens. Different designs of coops have different features, such as nesting boxes, roosts, feeders, waterers, windows, vents, doors, and ramps, and some may take up more or less space than others.

For example, a coop with nesting boxes and roosts inside the coop may need more floor space than one with nesting boxes and roosts outside the coop. On the other hand, a coop that has feeders and waterers inside may need less run space than a coop with feeders and waterers outside.

4. Coop location:

The location of your coop will also affect how much space you will need to provide for your chickens. Different locations of coops have different advantages and disadvantages, such as sunlight, drainage, wind, noise, and accessibility, and some may require more or less space than others.

For example, a coop in a sunny and well-drained area may need less insulation and ventilation than a coop in a shady and damp area. On the other hand, a coop located in a windy and noisy area may need more protection and security than a coop located in a calm and quiet area.

You can choose the best size for your chicken coop by considering these factors. You can also provide your chickens with a comfortable and secure home.

Ventilation

Ventilation is one of the most important aspects of your chicken coop, as it will provide your chickens with fresh air to breathe and regulate their body temperature. Ventilation will also prevent the buildup of moisture, ammonia, dust, and pathogens, which can cause respiratory problems, diseases, and infections for your chickens. Therefore, you will need to choose the best ventilation for your chicken coop based on the following factors:

1. **Airflow:**

You must ensure that your chicken coop has a good airflow, which means the air can enter and exit the coop freely and evenly. To create a cross-ventilation effect, you will need to install windows, vents, or fans in your coop, preferably on opposite sides or corners. You must also avoid blocking the airflow with objects like furniture, feeders, waterers, or nesting boxes.

2. **Air quality:**

You must ensure that your chicken coop has good air quality, which means the air is clean, dry, and odorless. You will need to keep your coop run clean and dry and remove any feces, bedding, feed, or water that are dirty or spoiled. You will also need to use bedding materials that are absorbent and dust-free, such as straw, shavings, or sand, and change them regularly.

3. **Air temperature:**

You must ensure that your chicken coop has a good air temperature, which means that the air is neither too hot nor too cold for your chickens.

You will need to insulate your coop by using materials such as wood, straw, or foam to keep your chickens warm in the winter and cool in the summer. You will also need to adjust the ventilation by opening or closing the windows, vents, or fans to regulate the temperature and humidity in your coop.

Choosing the best ventilation for your chicken coop can provide your chickens with a comfortable and healthy environment. You can also prevent and treat common chicken diseases and keep your flock healthy.

Insulation

Insulation is another important aspect of your chicken coop, as it will keep your chickens warm in the winter and cool in the summer. Insulation will also prevent the loss of heat and moisture, which can affect the comfort and health of your chickens. Therefore, you will need to choose the best insulation for your chicken coop based on the following factors:

1. Climate:

Your area's climate will determine how much and what kind of insulation you will need for your chicken coop. Different climates have different temperatures, humidity, and precipitation; some may require more or less insulation than others.

For example, if you live in a cold and snowy area, you will need more insulation to keep your chickens warm and dry. Living in a hot and humid area will require less insulation to keep your chickens cool and ventilated.

2. Material:

The material of your insulation will affect its effectiveness, durability, and cost. Different materials have different properties, such as thermal conductivity, water resistance, and fire resistance, and some may be more or less suitable than others.

For example, wood is a natural and cheap material that can provide some insulation. Still, it can also rot, mold, or burn. Straw is another natural and cheap material that can provide good insulation but also attract pests and parasites. Foam is a synthetic and expensive material that can provide excellent insulation but can also be toxic or flammable.

3. Installation:

Installing your insulation will affect its performance, maintenance, and appearance. Different installations have different methods, such as stapling, gluing, or spraying; some may be easier than others.

For example, stapling is a simple and quick method that can attach insulation to the walls and ceiling of your coop. Still, it can also leave gaps or holes that can reduce the insulation. Gluing is another simple and quick method that can attach insulation to the walls and ceiling of your coop.

Still, it can also be messy or sticky. Spraying is a complex and slow method that can cover the entire surface of your coop with insulation. Still, it can also be expensive or complicated.

By choosing the best insulation for your chicken coop, you can keep your chickens warm in the winter and cool in the summer. You will also be able to prevent the loss of heat and moisture and improve the comfort and health of your chickens.

Flooring

The flooring of your coop is another important aspect of your chicken coop, as it will affect your chickens' cleanliness, comfort, and health. The flooring of your coop will also affect the ease and frequency of your cleaning and maintenance. Therefore, you will need to choose the best flooring for your coop based on the following factors:

1. **Material:**

The material of your flooring will affect its durability, cost, and appearance. Different materials have different properties, such as water resistance, odor resistance, and heat retention, and some may be more or less suitable than others. For example, wood is a natural and cheap material that can provide some insulation and comfort.

Still, it can also rot, mold, or harbor parasites. Concrete is a synthetic and expensive material that can provide a solid and easy-to-clean surface. Still, it can also crack, absorb moisture, or become cold. Dirt is a natural and accessible material that can provide a soft and natural surface. Still, it can also become muddy, dusty, or uneven.

2. Bedding:

The bedding of your flooring will affect its absorbency, comfort, and appearance. Different beddings have different properties, such as dust level, odor level, and compostability, and some may be more or less suitable than others. For example, straw is a natural and cheap bedding that can provide good insulation and comfort.

Still, it can also be dusty, smelly, or flammable. Shavings are natural and cheap bedding that can provide good absorbency and comfort. Still, they can also be dusty, slippery, or hard to find. Sand is a natural and cheap bedding that can provide good drainage and comfort. Still, it can also be heavy, messy, or abrasive.

3. Maintenance:

The maintenance of your flooring will affect its performance, frequency, and ease. Different floorings have different maintenance needs, such as sweeping, raking, or shoveling, and some may be more or less easy than others.

For example, wood flooring may need to be swept daily and replaced annually to keep it clean and dry. Concrete flooring may need to be raked weekly and scrubbed monthly to keep it clean and odorless. Dirt flooring may need to be shoveled monthly and tilled annually to keep it level and fresh.

Choosing the best flooring for your coop will keep your chickens clean, comfortable, and healthy. You will also be able to make your cleaning and maintenance easier and more enjoyable.

Provision

Nesting boxes, roosts, feeders, and waterers are essential for the chickens in your coop. These items will ensure that your chickens have a comfortable and productive life. Here is how to provide these items for your chickens:

1. **Nesting boxes:**

Nesting boxes are cozy and private places where your chickens will lay their eggs. You must provide one nesting box for every three to four chickens and place them in a dark and quiet corner of your coop.

You will also need to make the nesting boxes at least 12 inches by 12 inches by 12 inches in size and line them with soft and clean bedding, such as straw, shavings, or hay. You must keep the nesting boxes clean and dry and collect the eggs daily.

2. Roosts:

Roosts are comfortable and secure places where your chickens will sleep at night. You must provide one roost for every chicken and place them at least 2 feet above the ground and 1 foot apart. You will also need to make the roosts at least 2 inches wide and 4 inches long and use smooth and sturdy materials, such as wood, metal, or PVC. You must also keep the roosts clean and dry and regularly remove droppings.

3. Feeders:

Feeders are containers where your chickens will eat their food. You must provide one feeder for every six to eight chickens and place them in a convenient and accessible location in your coop or run.

You will also need to make the feeders large enough to hold enough food for your chickens and use durable and easy-to-clean materials, such as metal, plastic, or ceramic. You must also keep the feeders clean and full, preventing waste or spillage.

4. Waterers:

Waterers are containers where your chickens will drink their water. You must provide one waterer for every six to eight chickens and place them in a convenient and accessible location in your coop or run. You will also need to make the waterers large enough to hold enough water for your chickens and use durable and easy-to-clean materials, such as metal, plastic, or ceramic. You must also keep the waterers clean and full and prevent freezing or contamination.

By providing these items for your chickens, you can keep them comfortable and productive. You will also enjoy the benefits of raising chickens, such as fresh eggs and meat.

Protect

Protecting your chickens from predators and intruders is one of the most crucial and challenging aspects of raising chickens. Predators and intruders can harm or kill your chickens or steal your eggs and meat. They can also cause stress, fear, and injury to your chickens and damage your coop and run.

Therefore, you will need to protect your chickens from predators and intruders by using the following methods:

1. Predator-proof your coop and run:

You must make your coop and run predator-proof, meaning no predator or intruder can enter or exit your coop and run without your permission.

You will need to:

- Use materials that are strong and durable, such as wood, metal, or wire, and secure them with nails, screws, or staples.

- Cover gaps or holes that may allow predators or intruders to enter or exit, such as windows, vents, doors, or ramps.

- Bury the wire or fence at least 12 inches deep or bend it outward at a 90-degree angle to prevent predators or intruders from digging under or climbing over your coop and running.

2. Deter or deal with predators and intruders:

You must deter or deal with predators or intruders that may try to attack or bother your chickens by using various methods, such as traps, alarms, lights, or dogs. You will need to identify the type and behavior of the predators or intruders and use the appropriate method accordingly. For example, if you have raccoons, which are nocturnal and clever, you may use traps, alarms, or lights to catch, scare, or repel them.

3. **Monitor your chickens and coop:**

You will need to monitor your chickens and coop regularly and closely and look for any signs or evidence of predators or intruders. You must

- Observe your chickens' behavior, appearance, and output and check for changes or abnormalities.

- Inspect your coop, run, and look for any damage or disturbance.

- Keep records of your chickens and coop and note any issues or incidents.

By protecting your chickens from predators and intruders, you will be able to keep your chickens safe and happy. You will also enjoy the benefits of raising chickens and avoiding risks or losses.

Chapter 3

How to Feed and Care for Your Chickens

After you have built a comfortable and secure chicken coop for your chickens, you will need to feed and care for your chickens. Feeding and caring for your chickens is one of the most essential and enjoyable aspects of raising chickens. It will give your chickens the nutrition, health, and happiness they need. It will also make your chicken adventure more rewarding and fun. In this chapter, you will learn how to feed and care for your chickens based on the following topics:

- What to feed your chickens and how much to ensure their optimal nutrition and well-being

- How to supplement your chickens' diet with vitamins, minerals, and herbs

- How to spoil your chickens with treats and snacks that they will love

- How to perform routine health checks and grooming for your chickens

By the end of this chapter, you will have a clear idea of how to feed and care for your chickens. You will be ready to start your feeding and caring routine and create a happy and healthy flock of chickens.

Nurturing Your Flock

Embarking on the chicken-keeping journey involves more than just providing shelter; it requires a keen understanding of what and how much to feed your feathered companions. Nutrition is the cornerstone for their energy, growth, and overall well-being, influencing their health, behavior, and appearance. Delve into the intricacies of ensuring optimal nutrition for your chickens and fostering their well-being through a thoughtful approach to feeding:

1. Layer Feed Essentials:

- **Nutrient-Rich Mainstay:** Layer feed is the primary sustenance for your chickens, encompassing vital nutrients like protein, calcium, and vitamins essential for egg production and overall health.

- **Daily Regimen:** Offering layer feed should be a daily practice, with free access provided to your chickens. The choice between pellets, crumbles, or mash depends on your flock's preferences.

- **Tailored Nutrition:** Adjust the quantity based on age, size, breed, and the prevailing season or climate. As a guideline, we aim to provide approximately 1/4 pound of layer feed per chicken per day to meet their dietary requirements.

2. Supplemental Grit Support:

- **Digestive Aid:** Grit serves as a valuable supplement, aiding in the digestion of grains, seeds, and grasses consumed by your chickens.

- **Weekly Inclusion:** Integrate grit into their diet weekly, ensuring free access. The choice between sand, oyster shells, or granite depends on the specific needs of your flock.

- **Tailored Application:** Adjust the amount of grit based on the food your chickens consume. Generally, aim for approximately 1 teaspoon of grit per chicken per week to facilitate optimal digestion.

3. Hydration Priority Water:

- **Essential Lifeline:** Water is the most vital component of your chickens' diet, ensuring hydration, temperature regulation, and support for bodily functions.

- **Daily Offering:** Provide water daily, offering unrestricted access. The type and quality of water, whether from the tap, well, or rain, should be selected based on your chickens' preferences.

- **Adaptive Hydration:** Adjust the water quantity in response to your flock's temperature, humidity, and activity level. A general guideline is to provide approximately 1 quart of water per chicken daily for sustained well-being.

By meticulously attending to the dietary needs of your chickens and tailoring their food options and quantities to their unique requirements, you ensure their optimal nutrition and lay the foundation for a thriving and contented flock. The rewards extend beyond sustenance, allowing you to relish the delights of fresh eggs and meat while fostering the well-being of your cherished feathered companions.

Elevating Chicken Well-Being

Beyond the staple diet for your chickens lies the opportunity to enhance their nutritional intake through thoughtfully chosen supplements. Including vitamins, minerals, and herbs not only augments their diet but also serves as a proactive measure in fortifying their immune system and warding off common diseases and parasites. Delve into the nuanced methods of supplementing your chickens' diet for optimal health and happiness:

1. Vitamin and Mineral Supplements:

- **Targeted Nutrient Boost:** Vitamin and mineral supplements offer concentrated doses of essential nutrients such as vitamin A, vitamin D, iron, and zinc, catering to the specific needs of your flock.

- **Applicability Across Life Stages:** Consider supplementing the diet, especially for young, elderly, ailing, stressed, or molting chickens. Choose from various forms, such as powder, liquid, or tablets, adapting to your chickens' preferences.

- **Tailored Administration:** Adjust the frequency and quantity based on guidelines provided on the label or advice from a veterinarian. Generally, supplementing with vitamin and mineral supplements once or twice a week, mixed with water or feed, proves beneficial for overall well-being.

2. Herbal Supplements:

- **Nature's Medicinal Bounty:** Herbal supplements harness the power of natural herbs like garlic, oregano, or thyme, offering medicinal and beneficial properties to support your chickens' health.

- **Targeted Use for Ailments:** Consider herbal supplements when addressing your flock's infections, inflammations, or parasitic concerns. Choose from fresh, dried, or oil-based supplements based on your chickens' preferences.

- **Personalized Dosage:** Tailor the amount and frequency of herbal supplements to your chickens' specific needs and conditions. Integrating herbal supplements into their diet once or twice a week, either in water or feed, can contribute to overall vitality.

By conscientiously incorporating vitamins, minerals, and herbs into your chickens' diet, you extend beyond basic sustenance, providing an enriched nutritional experience.

This practice offers additional nutrients and serves as a proactive measure, bolstering their immune defenses and mitigating common health challenges. The result is improved physical health and heightened happiness among your cherished flock.

Indulging Your Feathered Companions

Beyond daily sustenance and essential supplements, the opportunity to pamper your chickens with delectable treats and snacks awaits. While not essential, these indulgent offerings serve as a flavorful, fun, and rewarding addition to your chickens' diet. Delve into the delightful ways to spoil your feathered friends, providing them with variety, stimulation, and enrichment through the following methods:

1. Kitchen Scraps Extravaganza:

- **Residual Culinary Delights:** Kitchen scraps, remnants of your culinary endeavors, become a delightful treat for your chickens. Opt for fresh, organic, healthy options such as fruits, vegetables, bread, cheese, or meat.

- **Customized Selection:** Tailor the type and size of kitchen scraps to suit your chickens' preferences – whether it's the crunch of apples, the sweetness of carrots, or the satisfaction of corn. Adjust the quantity based on your chickens' appetite and preferences, spoiling them with kitchen scraps once or twice a day, scattered in their run or coop.

2. Garden Produce Galore:

- **Harvesting Nature's Bounty:** Elevate the treat experience by incorporating garden produce featuring herbs, flowers, or edible weeds. Select options that are colorful and aromatic but also safe and enjoyable for your chickens.

- **Seasonal Variety:** Choose garden produce based on the seasons and availability in your garden – whether it's the fragrant allure of basil, the vibrant hues of marigold, or the nutritional benefits of dandelion. Treat your chickens to produce from the garden once or twice a week, suspending them in their run or coop for added enrichment.

3. Commercial Treat Extravaganza:

- **Tailored Store-Bought Delicacies:** Explore the world of commercial treats explicitly designed for chickens, including mealworms, seeds, or pellets. Opt for high-quality, nutritious, and delicious options to spoil your chickens.

- **Diverse Forms:** Choose from various commercial treat forms, whether dried, live, or mixed, catering to your chickens' preferences. Adjust the quantity and frequency based on the cost and convenience of the product, treating your chickens to these delights once or twice a month, scattered in their run or coop.

You go beyond mere sustenance by indulging your chickens with treats and snacks they adore, providing them with a sensory experience that enhances their lives. This practice introduces variety, stimulation, and enrichment. It fosters a deeper bond between you and your feathered companions, ensuring their happiness and contentment.

Caring for Your Feathered Friends

Beyond providing food and shelter, another critical aspect of responsible chicken ownership involves the regular performance of health checks and grooming. These practices allow you to monitor your chickens' well-being and contribute to maintaining their health, hygiene, and overall appearance. By incorporating the following detailed methods into your routine, you can effectively prevent and address common issues that may impact your cherished flock:

1. Weekly Health Checks:

- **Thorough Physical Assessment:** Health checks entail a weekly examination to assess your chickens' physical and mental condition. During this process, diligently observe for signs of illness, injury, or stress.

- **Comprehensive Evaluation:** Inspect their eyes, ears, nose, mouth, feathers, skin, legs, feet, and vent for abnormalities. Be vigilant for indications such as discharge, swelling, bleeding, scabs, lice, mites, worms, diarrhea, lameness, deformity, or changes in behavior.

- **Weighing and Documentation:** Regularly weigh your chickens and maintain detailed records of their weight and any identified issues or treatments. This meticulous approach aids in tracking their health trends over time.

2. Monthly Grooming Sessions:

- **Hygiene and Appearance Maintenance:** Grooming sessions, scheduled monthly or as needed, focus on preserving and enhancing the hygiene and appearance of your chickens.

- **Parasite and Debris Removal:** Thoroughly inspect and remove any dirt, debris, or parasites from their feathers, skin, legs, feet, and vent. This not only enhances cleanliness but also prevents potential health issues.

- **Trimming Nails, Beaks, and Wings:** Address overgrown or sharp nails, beaks, and wings that may pose problems for your chickens or you. Regular trimming ensures their comfort and prevents unintended complications.

- **Bathing When Necessary:** Bathing becomes essential if your chickens appear excessively dirty or emit unpleasant odors. Ensure a gentle and thorough cleansing process, followed by meticulous drying to prevent discomfort.

By integrating routine health checks and grooming into your chicken care regimen, you actively contribute to the well-being of your flock. Monitoring, maintaining, and enhancing their health, hygiene, and appearance become a responsibility and a gesture of genuine care. This proactive approach equips you with the tools to prevent and address common challenges, fostering a thriving and contented community of chickens under your care.

Chapter 4

How to Collect and Store Fresh Eggs

One of the main reasons to raise chickens is to enjoy fresh eggs from your backyard. Fresh eggs are delicious but also nutritious, healthy, and economical. However, to enjoy the full benefits of fresh eggs, you must collect and store them properly. In this chapter, you will learn how to collect and store fresh eggs based on the following topics:

- When and how to collect eggs from your chickens
- How to clean and grade eggs according to size and quality
- How to store eggs for maximum freshness and safety

- How to use and cook eggs in delicious recipes

By the end of this chapter, you will have a clear idea of how to collect and store fresh eggs.

Harvesting the Fruits of Chicken Keeping

Engaging in the gratifying task of collecting eggs from your feathered companions is undeniably one of the highlights of raising chickens. It brings a sense of accomplishment and satisfaction and fosters a connection of gratitude with your flock.

To master the art of egg collection, understanding the when and how is crucial. Here's a comprehensive guide to assist you:

1. Optimal Timing for Egg Collection:

- **Daily Ritual:** Make it a daily practice to collect eggs from your chickens, ideally in the morning and evening. This routine ensures you gather the freshest and most abundant eggs, minimizing the risk of spoilage, damage, or theft.

- **Weather Considerations:** Stay attuned to the weather and seasonal variations. In extreme conditions – whether it's too hot, cold, wet, or dry – consider increasing the frequency of egg collection. This proactive approach safeguards against issues like cracking, freezing, or molding.

2. Best Practices for Egg Collection:

- **Gentle and Careful Approach:** Approach the egg collection process with gentleness and care to avoid causing stress, injury, or disturbance to your chickens. A calm demeanor contributes to a positive environment for you and your flock.

- **Appropriate Containers:** Use a suitable container, such as a basket, bucket, or bag, to hold the eggs during collection. Line the container with a soft and clean material like straw, shavings, or paper towels to ensure the eggs are cushioned and protected.

- **Hygiene Measures:** Prioritize hygiene by wearing gloves or washing your hands before and after collecting eggs. This practice minimizes the risk of contamination or infection and maintains the overall cleanliness of the eggs.

- **Respectful Interaction:** Exercise patience and respect when collecting eggs, avoiding aggression or interference with your chickens' nesting behavior. A harmonious and considerate approach contributes to a positive relationship between you and your flock.

By collecting eggs daily with care and consideration, you reap the rewards of fresh eggs and nurture a positive connection with your chickens. This shared routine becomes a bonding experience, enhancing the joy and contentment within your chicken-keeping journey.

Elevating Egg Management

In chicken keeping, the essential task of cleaning and grading eggs stands out as a crucial and valuable practice. Beyond ensuring cleanliness, this process plays a pivotal role in enhancing the quality and appearance of your eggs, allowing for effective sorting and organization based on your specific requirements. Here's an in-depth guide on how to meticulously clean and grade eggs, factoring in size and quality:

1. Masterful Egg Cleaning Techniques:

- **Timely Cleaning:** Initiate the cleaning process promptly after eggs are laid, aiming to remove any dirt, debris, or stains from the shells. Timeliness is key to maintaining the integrity of the eggs.

Choosing the Right Method:

- **Dry Method:** Employ a brush, cloth, or sandpaper to eliminate dirt or debris from the shells gently. This method is suitable for eggs with dry or adherent contaminants.

- **Wet Method:** Utilize warm water, a mild soap, or a vinegar solution for eggs with stains or potential bacterial presence.

Ensure a gentle wash and thorough drying to prevent cracking or excessive shell moisture.

2. Precision in Grading Eggs:

Size Assessment:

- **Utilize Measurement Tools:** Employ scales, rulers, or charts to measure the weight and length of each egg. Based on these measurements, categorize eggs into small, medium, large, or extra-large sizes.

Quality Inspection:

- **Candling Process:** Illuminate the egg's interior using a candling device, flashlight, or lamp to identify defects such as blood spots, meat spots, or cracks. This step ensures the overall quality and integrity of each egg.

Effective Storage and Labeling:

- **Utilize Containers:** Choose appropriate containers, whether cartons, trays, or baskets, to store graded eggs. Ensure proper labeling, including the respective chickens' date, grade, and name.

By embracing the practices of cleaning and grading eggs meticulously, you not only enhance the hygiene, quality, and appearance of your eggs but also streamline their organization based on your unique needs. This conscientious approach contributes to a rewarding and efficient egg management system within your chicken-keeping venture.

Preserving Freshness and Safety

Navigating the intricacies of storing eggs harvested from your feathered companions is a pivotal yet challenging task in chicken keeping.

How you store eggs significantly impacts their freshness, safety, and overall quality, influencing taste, texture, and color. Mastering the art of proper egg storage is essential. Here's a comprehensive guide to help you achieve maximum freshness and safety for your eggs:

1. Refrigeration Mastery for Long-Term Freshness:

- **Appropriate Containers:** Utilize cartons, trays, or baskets for egg storage within the refrigerator. These containers help maintain organization and protect the eggs from potential damage.

- **Strategic Placement:** Store eggs in the middle or back of the refrigerator, where the temperature is more stable and cooler. This ensures a consistent environment, preserving the freshness of the eggs over an extended period.

- **Correct Orientation:** Keep eggs in their original position, with the pointed end down and the round end up. This safeguards against air entering the shells, preserving the eggs' quality.

- **Avoiding Detrimental Factors:** Steer clear of strong odors, excess moisture, or exposure to light within the refrigerator. These factors can lead to spoilage, discoloration, or deterioration of the eggs.

2. Room Temperature Storage for Short-Term Freshness:

- **Appropriate Vessels:** Choose baskets, bowls, or racks suited for egg storage at room temperature. These containers should be placed in a cool and dry location, away from heat, sunlight, or humidity.

- **Optimal Placement:** Position the eggs away from heat, sunlight, or humidity sources to maintain their quality. Ensure they are stored in their original orientation, with the pointed end down and the round end up.

- **Guarding Against Contaminants:** Be vigilant about the cleanliness of the storage area, preventing dust, insects, or rodents from compromising the integrity of the eggs.

By meticulously adhering to these storage practices, you extend the freshness and safety of your eggs and guarantee a delightful and risk-free egg-eating experience. Embrace these strategies to savor the full benefits of fresh eggs while minimizing any potential risks or losses in your chicken-keeping journey.

Epicurean Adventures

Embarking on the culinary journey of using and cooking eggs from your cherished flock is a culinary escapade and the epitome of joy and reward in chicken keeping. This gastronomic exploration allows you to relish your freshly laid eggs' distinctive taste, texture, and color while crafting delectable recipes to tantalize your taste buds and those of your loved ones. Delve into the world of culinary creativity with these detailed tips on how to use and cook eggs in delightful recipes:

1. Maximizing Egg Usage:

Optimal Timing: Utilize eggs promptly to savor their unparalleled freshness and quality. Align the usage with their size and grade, selecting the appropriate eggs for different recipes and portion sizes.

Temperature Consideration: Factor in the temperature and age of the eggs when incorporating them into your culinary endeavors. Employ cold and fresh eggs for baking while reserving room temperature and older eggs for boiling or frying.

2. Culinary Precision in Egg Cooking:

Gentle and Careful Cooking: Approach egg cooking with a gentle and careful touch, steering clear of overcooking, undercooking, or burning. Preserve the delicate textures and flavors inherent in freshly laid eggs.

Optimal Tools and Techniques: Equip yourself with the right tools and techniques tailored to each type of egg dish. Utilize low to medium heat, a nonstick pan, a spatula, and a timer for precise and efficient cooking.

Seasoning Expertise: Elevate your egg creations' flavor profile and visual appeal by incorporating the right seasonings and accompaniments. Experiment with various flavors to discover enticing combinations that complement the unique qualities of your farm-fresh eggs.

By immersing yourself in the art of using and cooking eggs from your cherished chickens, you not only relish the distinctive qualities of your fresh eggs but also unleash your culinary creativity. This exploration opens the door to a world of culinary possibilities, allowing you to experiment with diverse cuisines, ingredients, and methods while creating memorable and delicious recipes for your family.

Chapter 5

How to Raise Meat Chickens

Another reason to raise chickens is to produce meat for consumption or sale. Meat chickens are raised for their meat rather than their eggs. Raising meat chickens can be rewarding and profitable, as you can enjoy fresh, healthy, and tasty chicken meat from your backyard.

However, raising meat chickens can also be challenging and demanding, as you must provide them with special care, feed, and equipment. In this chapter, you will learn how to raise meat chickens based on the following topics:

- The advantages and disadvantages of raising meat chickens
- How to select and raise the best breeds for meat production

- How to store and cook chicken meat in mouth-watering dishes

By the end of this chapter, you will have a clear idea of how to raise meat chickens and enjoy the benefits of raising meat chickens.

Pros and Cons

Embarking on raising meat chickens involves a nuanced evaluation of its advantages and disadvantages, demanding careful consideration before taking the plunge. Here is a comprehensive overview of the pros and cons associated with raising meat chickens:

<u>Advantages</u>

1. Freshness:

Revel delight in consuming freshly harvested chicken meat from your homestead, mitigating concerns associated with the age, freezing, or contamination often found in market-sourced poultry.

2. Quality Control:

Exercise precise control over the quality of your chicken meat, ensuring it attains the highest standards of health, nutrition, and flavor. You guarantee a premium product by offering superior care, feed, and living conditions.

3. Economic Benefits:

Realize substantial savings by producing chicken meat, circumventing the escalating costs of purchasing commercial meat. Additionally, you have the potential to generate income by selling surplus chicken meat to a local clientele.

4. Satisfaction and Pride:

Experience a profound sense of satisfaction, accomplishment, and pride by actively participating in raising and providing for your family through chicken meat production.

Disadvantages

1. Time Commitment:

Raising meat chickens demands significant time and effort. The additional care, specialized feed, and equipment required, coupled with the time-consuming process of slaughtering and processing, can pose challenges.

2. Space Requirements:

Adequate space is crucial for successfully rearing meat chickens, as they require more room for growth and exercise than their egg-laying counterparts. Furthermore, a suitable area for the messy and odorous slaughtering and processing phase is imperative.

3. Financial Considerations:

The financial commitment to raising meat chickens is substantial, encompassing increased feed, water, and electricity costs. Additional investments in specialized equipment such as brooders, feeders, waterers, and pluckers contribute to the overall expense.

4. Emotional Challenges:

The emotional aspects of raising meat chickens can be complex, involving potential attachment, feelings of guilt, or grief as you raise, slaughter, and consume or sell your chickens.

By thoroughly examining the advantages and disadvantages of raising meat chickens, you empower yourself to make an informed decision aligned with your resources, goals, and ethical considerations. This comprehensive analysis prepares you for the multifaceted challenges and rewards inherent in the pursuit of raising meat chickens.

Navigating the Complexities

Choosing and nurturing the most suitable breeds for meat production is a pivotal and intricate facet of raising chickens. Distinct breeds exhibit varying traits, encompassing growth rate, feed conversion, meat quality, and disease resistance, necessitating a judicious selection based on several crucial factors. To embark on this journey, one must meticulously evaluate the following elements:

★ **Factors Influencing Breed Selection:**

1. Type of Meat Chicken:

Broilers: Primarily raised for their breast meat, broilers face slaughter at a tender age, typically between 6 to 8 weeks.

Roasters: Sought for their whole-body meat, roasters undergo slaughter at a more mature age, generally around 12 to 16 weeks. The selection between these two types hinges on personal preferences, budget considerations, and market demands.

2. Breed of Meat Chicken:

Research and Comparison: Conduct thorough research and comparative analysis of various meat chicken breeds, including purebred and hybrid varieties.

Traits to Consider: Scrutinize traits such as size, weight, color, shape, flavor, and texture associated with each breed.

Requirements: Delve into specific breed requirements encompassing feed preferences, water needs, space considerations, and necessary equipment.

Availability and Cost: Factor in breed availability, overall cost implications, and popularity within the market.

★ Prominent Meat Chicken Breeds:

1. Cornish Cross:

Hybrid Breed: Widely acclaimed as the predominant choice for meat production.

Advantages: Exhibits a rapid growth rate, high feed conversion, and substantial breast meat.

Drawbacks: Tends to possess a lower disease resistance, elevated mortality rates, and a relatively bland flavor.

2. Freedom Ranger:

Hybrid Alternative: Presents an alternative to the Cornish Cross breed.

Characteristics: Features a slower growth rate, reduced feed conversion, and a smaller breast meat.

Benefits: Boasts higher disease resistance, lower mortality rates, and a richer flavor profile.

3. Heritage:

Purebred Traditional Breeds: Revered for their historical significance in meat production.

Attributes: Showcases a markedly slow growth rate, minimal feed conversion, and a modest breast meat portion.

Distinctive Advantages: Boasts exceptional disease resistance, low mortality rates, and a uniquely robust flavor.

★ **Strategic Considerations:**

Tailored Approach: Tailor your breed selection to align with your specific objectives, personal consumption, or commercial sale.

Optimizing Quality and Quantity: Strive to achieve a balance that optimizes the quality and quantity of chicken meat produced.

Risk Mitigation: Thoroughly understanding and selecting breeds that align with your resources and goals helps avoid potential risks or losses associated with raising meat chickens.

In adopting a meticulous approach to selecting and raising meat chicken breeds, you empower yourself to navigate the intricacies of this complex undertaking. This comprehensive guide prepares you for the multifaceted challenges and rewards of pursuing optimal meat chicken production.

Mastering the Art of Storing and Cooking Chicken

Embarking on a culinary journey with chicken opens the door to a world of mouth-watering possibilities. To ensure a delightful experience from kitchen to table, mastering the art of storing and cooking chicken is paramount. With these affirmative and expert techniques, you will elevate your culinary prowess, transforming simple chicken into savory masterpieces.

Storing Chicken: A Fresh Start for Culinary Excellence

1. Discerning Selection:

Kickstart your culinary adventure by choosing quality chicken. Opt for fresh, locally sourced poultry for the best flavor and texture. A keen inspection of color and smell ensures freshness and culinary success.

2. Chilled Perfection:

Upon acquiring your chicken, promptly refrigerate it at or below 40°F (4°C). For extended storage, utilize airtight containers or freezer bags. Leak-proof packaging prevents cross-contamination and preserves optimal freshness.

3. Organized Refrigeration:

Strategically place raw chicken on the bottom shelf of the refrigerator to prevent juices from impacting other foods. Maintain it in its original packaging or position it on a plate to capture potential leaks.

4. Thawing Safely:

When thawing frozen chicken, opt for the refrigerator, microwave, or a sealed plastic bag submerged in cold water. Avoid room temperature thawing to mitigate the risk of bacterial growth.

5. Timely Utilization or Freezing:

Fresh chicken should ideally be consumed within 1–2 days, ensuring peak quality. Frozen chicken, stored at 0°F (-18°C), boasts a 9–12 months lifespan. Methodically label packages with dates for streamlined tracking.

<u>Cooking Techniques</u>

1. Marination Alchemy:

Elevate flavor profiles by marinating chicken before cooking. Craft a tantalizing blend of herbs, spices, oils, and acids to infuse the meat with rich tastes. Allow for a minimum of 30 minutes for optimal flavor penetration.

2. Roasting Brilliance:

For succulent whole chickens or larger cuts, roasting is a timeless technique. Preheat the oven, season the chicken, and roast until the internal temperature reaches 165°F (74°C). Basting during cooking enhances juiciness.

3. Grilling Mastery:

Achieve a delightful smoky essence with grilling. Preheat the grill, season the chicken, and cook until the internal temperature reaches the safe zone. Grill marks and a smoky aroma heighten the overall experience.

4. Pan-Seared Excellence:

Ideal for quick and flavorful results, pan-searing involves heating a skillet, searing the chicken until golden brown, and finishing it in the oven. This method locks in juices and creates a **delectable crust.**

5. Simmering Comfort:

Create comforting stews, soups, or braises by simmering chicken in flavorful liquids. This slow-cooking method yields tender and juicy meat, perfect for chilly evenings.

6. Crispy Fried Delight:

For crispy textures, frying is the path to golden-brown perfection. Whether deep or shallow, ensuring the oil is hot before adding the chicken guarantees a crispy outcome.

7. Slow Cooking Versatility:

Embrace the convenience and tenderness of slow cookers. Combine seasoned chicken, vegetables, and broth for an effortlessly mouth-watering meal.

8. Pressure Cooking Innovation:

The pressure cooker emerges as a time-saving marvel, delivering perfectly cooked chicken in a fraction of the time while preserving moisture and flavor.

Serve and Savor: Bringing Chicken Delights to the Table

1. Post-Cooking Rest:

Allow cooked chicken to rest for a few minutes before slicing or serving. This crucial step ensures the redistribution of juices, resulting in a moist and flavorful bite.

2. Garnish and Presentation:

Elevate the visual appeal of your chicken dishes with garnishes. Fresh herbs, citrus slices, or a sauce drizzle add flavor and aesthetic charm.

3. Pairing Perfection:

Choose complementary sides to accompany your chicken dish. Whether it's a crisp salad, flavorful rice, or roasted vegetables, thoughtful pairings enhance the overall dining experience.

4. Creative Leftovers:

Transform leftover chicken into new culinary delights. Incorporate shredded chicken into salads, sandwiches, or wraps for quick and tasty meals.

By following these meticulously crafted techniques for storing and cooking chicken, you are guaranteed to unlock a world of culinary delights. From the freshness of your ingredients to the precision of your cooking methods, each step contributes to mouth-watering dishes that will leave a lasting impression on your taste buds. Enjoy the journey of creating and savoring delicious chicken masterpieces in your kitchen.

Chapter 6

How to Hatch and Raise Baby Chicks

One of the most exciting and rewarding aspects of raising chickens is to hatch and raise baby chicks. Baby chicks are adorable, fluffy, and lively creatures that will bring you joy and happiness. However, hatching and raising baby chicks can also be challenging and demanding, as you must provide them with the best care, environment, and equipment. You will also need to monitor their growth, development, and health. In this chapter, you will learn how to hatch and raise baby chicks based on the following topics:

★ How to incubate eggs or use a broody hen to hatch your chicks

- ★ How to care for newly hatched chicks and provide them with warmth, food, and water

- ★ How to raise baby chicks and provide them with space, light, and protection

- ★ How to deal with common problems and challenges that may affect your baby chicks

By the end of this chapter, you will have a clear idea of how to hatch, raise baby chicks and be ready to start your hatching and raising adventure and enjoy the benefits of baby chicks.

Mastering Chick Hatching

Embarking on the journey of hatching your chicks is an engaging and captivating process that unveils the miracle of life. This exciting endeavor presents two primary methods:

incubating eggs or utilizing a broody hen. Choosing between these methods requires consideration of your preferences, budget, and availability. The following steps outline how to successfully incubate eggs or use a broody hen to hatch your chicks:

Incubating Eggs: Precision and Control

1. Selecting Eggs:

Begin by carefully choosing fertile, fresh, and clean eggs. Opt for the right size, shape, and color, avoiding cracks or dirt. Mark the eggs with relevant information such as date, breed, and parentage.

2. Incubator Setup:

Ensure your chosen incubator is clean, dry, and stable. Select an incubator with features such as temperature, humidity, ventilation controls, and turning mechanisms. Test and adjust the incubator to optimal settings based on manual instructions or expert advice.

3. Placing Eggs in the Incubator:

Arrange eggs to allow sufficient space and air circulation, preventing crowding or contact. Turn the eggs manually or automatically at least twice daily, rotating them 180 degrees to prevent sticking or deformation.

4. Monitoring Eggs in the Incubator:

Regularly check for changes or issues while maintaining ideal temperature, humidity, and ventilation levels. Use a candling device, flashlight, or lamp to inspect the eggs weekly for signs of development, such as veins, air cells, or movement.

5. Hatching in the Incubator:

Cease egg turning three days before the expected hatch date. Increase humidity and ventilation to aid chicks in breaking out of their shells. Allow chicks to remain in the incubator until they are dry and fluffy, minimizing any disturbance to preserve heat and moisture.

Using a Broody Hen: Natural Simplicity

1. Selecting the Hen:

Choose a broody, healthy, and friendly hen for a natural hatching process. Ensure the selected hen matches the desired breed, age, and size, avoiding those too young, too old, or of improper size. Label the hen for easy identification.

2. Nest Setup:

Create a clean, dry, and comfortable nest in a suitable location. Opt for a nest that provides the necessary warmth and contact, avoiding exposure or inadequate space. Line the nest with soft materials like straw, shavings, or hay, changing them regularly.

3. Placing Eggs Under the Hen:

Gently place eggs under the hen, ensuring she accepts and covers them. Arrange the eggs to provide warmth and contact, avoiding those that might become too cold or dislodged. Allow the hen to perform her natural incubation duties undisturbed, intervening only when feeding, watering, or checks are necessary.

4. Monitoring Eggs Under the Hen:

Regularly observe the eggs under the broody hen, maintaining her health and happiness by providing adequate food, water, and security. Use a candling device, flashlight, or lamp weekly to check for signs of development, such as veins, air cells, or movement.

5. Hatching Under the Hen:

Allow the broody hen to complete the hatching process, ensuring the safety, health, and bonding of both the hen and the chicks. Remove unhatched or deceased eggs and refrain from interfering with or separating the hen and chicks to prevent stress or rejection.

You can successfully hatch your chicks by following these meticulously outlined steps for incubating eggs or utilizing a broody hen. Enjoy the fascination and joy of witnessing the hatching process and prepare yourself for the rewarding next step of raising these adorable baby chicks.

Newly Hatched Chicks

Ensuring the well-being of newly hatched chicks is a critical and intricate task in the early stages of raising these delicate creatures. The vulnerability and dependence of these chicks necessitate meticulous attention and thoughtful care. Despite the challenges, caring for newly hatched chicks is deeply rewarding, providing an opportunity to foster a strong bond and witness their growth. This comprehensive guide outlines the intricate details of caring for newly hatched chicks, focusing on warmth, nutrition, and hydration.

Providing Optimal Warmth: A Vital Element

1. Selection of Heat Source:

Choose a suitable heat source to create a warm and secure environment for your newly hatched chicks. Options include a reliable heat lamp, a heating pad designed for chicks, or a well-designed brooder with adjustable temperature controls.

2. Temperature Considerations:

Recognize the vulnerability of newly hatched chicks to temperature fluctuations. Maintain an initial temperature of around 95°F (35°C) during the first week, gradually reducing it by 5°F (2.8°C) each subsequent week until the chicks are fully feathered. Utilize a thermometer, thermostat, or keen observation to ensure the optimal temperature, adjusting as needed.

3. **Monitoring Signs of Discomfort:**

Regularly observe your chicks for signs of discomfort or stress. Indicators such as huddling together, excessive panting, or constant peeping can suggest that the temperature is too high or too low. Swift adjustments to the heat source should be made to address these concerns promptly.

<u>Ensuring Adequate Nutrition</u>

1. **Feeding Frequency:**

Understand the high frequency and regularity with which newly hatched chicks must be fed. Establish a feeding routine, offering small daily meals to prevent starvation and promote healthy growth.

2. Feeder Selection:

Choose appropriate feeders, dishes, or trays that facilitate easy access to the specially formulated starter feed. Opt for a high-protein and high-quality starter feed, considering medicated or organic options for enhanced health benefits.

3. Supplemental Grit Usage:

Introduce grit, sand, or crushed shells into the feeding regimen to aid digestion. This supplemental element supports the chicks in breaking down and absorbing essential nutrients from their food.

Ensuring Hydration: A Vital Element of Chick Care

1. Water Source and Accessibility:

Provide a consistent and accessible water source for the newly hatched chicks. Use clean and shallow waterers that prevent drowning and encourage easy access for the chicks.

2. Hydration Frequency:

Recognize the susceptibility of chicks to dehydration and ensure a consistent supply of fresh water. Monitor the water level regularly, and clean and replenish as needed to maintain optimal hydration.

3. Electrolyte Considerations:

Consider adding electrolytes to the water during the initial days to boost hydration and essential nutrients. This is particularly beneficial during stressful periods or adverse weather conditions.

By meticulously following these detailed steps for warmth provision, nutritional care, and hydration management, you will be equipped to navigate the intricacies of caring for newly hatched chicks. The careful balance of warmth, sustenance, and hydration contributes to the health, vitality, and, ultimately, the successful growth of these charming chicks.

Minimizing Stress and Ensuring Harmony

The introduction of chicks to an existing flock is a pivotal yet challenging phase in the process of raising baby chicks. These vulnerable and timid creatures can face potential harm from older and stronger chickens, making a careful and gradual introduction imperative to avoid conflicts and ensure the safety of the entire flock.

This comprehensive guide provides detailed steps for introducing chicks to the rest of the flock while minimizing stress and potential conflicts.

Preparation for Chicks: A Crucial Foundation

1. Optimal Age and Feathering:

Wait until the chicks reach a minimum age of 8 weeks and achieve full feathering before introducing them to the older chickens. This ensures they can regulate their body temperature and withstand environmental conditions.

2. Wing Clipping:

Consider clipping chicks' wings, particularly if they are flighty or have excessively long wings. This preventative measure reduces the risk of chicks escaping or encountering trouble within the flock.

Flock Preparation

1. Understanding Flock Dynamics:

Observe the existing flock closely to discern the older chickens' pecking order, personalities, and behaviors. Identify any signs of aggression, dominance, or curiosity within the group.

2. Resource Provision:

Ensure the entire flock has abundant essential resources such as food, water, space, and roosts. This helps prevent competition, crowding, or stress during the introduction process.

Building Familiarity

1. Utilize Barriers:

Separate the chicks from the existing flock using barriers such as wire fences, crates, or cages.

Place them in proximity within the same area, such as the run or coop, for at least one week.

2. Sensory Familiarity:

Allow the chicks and the older chickens to see, hear, and smell each other through the barrier. Monitor their reactions, noting any signs of interest, indifference, or hostility, and adjust the proximity and duration of the introduction accordingly.

Ensuring a Smooth Transition

1. Timely Introduction:

Introduce the chicks to the flock fully once they have become familiar and comfortable with each other. Preferably conduct the introduction in the morning when older chickens are occupied and calm.

2. Supervised Interaction:

Remove the barrier and allow the chicks to mingle and interact with the flock. Maintain close supervision, observing for any conflicts such as pecking, chasing, or fighting. Intervene only if necessary, using separation, distraction, or relocation measures.

By meticulously following these comprehensive steps, introducing chicks to the rest of the flock can be navigated with care and expertise. This approach minimizes conflicts and stress and fosters a harmonious and contented flock of chickens.

Chapter 7
Solution

Raising chickens is a rewarding and enjoyable venture but has problems and challenges. Chickens are living creatures facing various issues, such as pests, parasites, diseases, injuries, or behavioral problems.

These issues can affect your chickens' health, happiness, and productivity and cause you stress, frustration, and loss. Therefore, you will need to solve common problems and challenges that may arise when raising chickens based on the following topics:

- How to deal with pests and parasites that can harm your chickens
- How to handle aggressive or bullying behavior among your chickens

- How to prevent and treat common diseases and injuries that can affect your chickens

- How to cope with environmental and seasonal changes that can impact your chickens

By the end of this chapter, you will have a clear idea of how to solve common problems and challenges that may arise when raising chickens.

Managing Pests and Parasites in Your Chicken Flock

Addressing pests and parasites is crucial to maintaining a healthy and thriving chicken flock. These unwelcome organisms, such as lice, mites, worms, fleas, or ticks, can lead to discomfort, diseases, and various health issues for your chickens. Preventive measures and targeted treatments are essential to deal with pests and parasites effectively. Here's a detailed guide on managing these challenges:

Preventive Measures: Building a Defense Shield

1. Maintain Cleanliness:

Regularly clean and dry your chicken coop and surrounding areas to eliminate potential habitats for pests and parasites. Remove dirt, debris, and moisture, which can attract and harbor these unwanted organisms.

2. Nutrition and Supplementation:

Provide your chickens with a well-balanced and nutritious diet. Consider supplementing their feed with vitamins, minerals, and herbs known for boosting immune system function. A robust immune system helps chickens resist infestations and infections.

3. Quarantine Protocol:

Implement a strict quarantine protocol for new or sick chickens. Before introducing them to the flock, inspect them for signs of pests and parasites. This step helps prevent the introduction of unwanted organisms to your existing flock.

Treatment Strategies: Eliminating Pests and Parasites

1. Identify and Assess:

Regularly inspect your chickens for signs of infestation, such as itching, irritation, or weight loss. Identify the pests or parasites affecting your flock to determine the most effective treatment approach.

2. Use Veterinary-Approved Products:

Choose appropriate products for treating your chickens, such as sprays, powders, or tablets. Veterinary-approved treatments are effective and safe. Follow the instructions on the label or seek advice from a veterinarian to ensure correct application.

3. Environmental Disinfection:

Disinfect the chicken coop and run using suitable products like bleach, vinegar, or diatomaceous earth. Consider the material and condition of your coop when choosing a disinfectant. Regular disinfection helps prevent reinfestation and creates an inhospitable environment for pests.

4. Integrated Pest Management (IPM):

Adopt an integrated approach that combines various strategies, such as biological controls, habitat modification, and chemical treatments.

This holistic approach ensures a more effective and sustainable pest and parasite management solution.

Monitoring and Evaluation: Ensuring Long-Term Success

1. Regular Checks:

Monitor your flock for any signs of recurring infestations or infections. Regular checks help detect issues early, allowing for prompt intervention.

2. Adapt Strategies:

Be flexible in your approach based on seasonal changes, environmental conditions, and the overall health of your flock. Adapt your strategies to address specific challenges and emerging issues.

You'll effectively manage pests and parasites in your chicken flock by implementing preventive measures and targeted treatments. This proactive approach safeguards your chickens from potential problems and diseases and contributes to their overall well-being and vitality.

Managing Aggressive Behavior in Your Chicken Flock

Addressing aggression or bullying among chickens is crucial for maintaining a harmonious and healthy flock. Such behavior can lead to stress, injuries, and disruptions within the flock dynamics. Effectively handling these situations requires a systematic approach that involves identification, intervention, and ongoing management. Here's a detailed guide to help you manage aggressive behavior in your chickens:

<u>Identification: Understanding the Root Causes</u>

1. Observation and Analysis:

Carefully observe your chickens to identify the aggressor, the victim, and the triggers for aggressive behavior—note patterns such as the time of day, specific locations, or frequency of incidents. Consider individual factors like breed, gender, age, personality, and environmental factors like available resources (food, water, space, roosts).

2. Identify Resource Competition:

Determine if aggressive behavior is triggered by resource competition, such as limited access to food, water, or space. Ensure that your coop and run are adequately equipped with resources to minimize competition.

3. Health Assessment:

Rule out health issues contributing to aggressive behavior. Injuries, illnesses, or discomfort can sometimes lead to aggressive behavior. Consult with a veterinarian if needed.

Intervention: Restoring Harmony in the Flock

1. Separation of Aggressor:

Temporarily separate the aggressive chicken from the flock to reduce immediate tension. Use a separate pen or enclosure, ensuring the isolated chicken can access food, water, and shelter.

2. Distraction Techniques:

Implement distraction techniques to redirect aggressive behavior. This can include introducing new items in the environment, rearranging the layout of the coop, or providing additional enrichment activities to keep chickens occupied.

3. Relocation of Resources:

Spread resources such as feeding stations, waterers, and roosts throughout the coop to prevent crowding and competition. This can help reduce triggers for aggression related to resource scarcity.

4. Behavior Modification Tools:

Utilize tools like spray bottles, noisemakers, or nets to interrupt aggressive behavior without causing harm. Consistency is key to reinforcing positive behavior.

Ongoing Management: Creating a Positive Flock Environment

1. Regular Monitoring:

Continue to observe the flock regularly to ensure that aggressive behavior does not recur. Be proactive in identifying signs of tension or stress.

2. Space Optimization:

Evaluate the space available to your chickens in the coop and the run. Sufficient space minimizes territorial disputes and reduces the likelihood of aggressive encounters.

3. Behavioral Enrichment:

Introduce environmental enrichment such as perches, dust baths, or hanging treats. This can divert their attention and provide positive outlets for natural behaviors.

4. Introduce New Members Strategically:

If adding new chickens to the flock, do so gradually and under supervision. Monitor interactions closely to ensure a smooth integration.

5. Professional Guidance:

Seek advice from poultry experts or a veterinarian if aggressive behavior persists or intensifies. They can provide additional insights and recommend specific strategies tailored to your flock.

By adopting a comprehensive approach that involves identification, intervention, and ongoing management, you can effectively handle aggressive behavior within your chicken flock. This promotes a positive and cooperative environment, ensuring the well-being of your feathered companions.

Molting and Egg-Laying Challenges Management

Addressing molting and egg-laying issues is pivotal for maintaining the well-being and productivity of your chicken flock. These natural processes, while essential, can pose challenges such as stress, reduced egg production, and discomfort for your feathered companions. Employing comprehensive strategies to cope with molting and egg-laying issues ensures that your chickens navigate these phases with optimal care. Here's a detailed guide to help you manage these challenges effectively:

Coping with Molting: Supporting Feather Regrowth

1. Nutritional Support:

Enhance your chickens' diet during molting to provide essential nutrients necessary for feather regrowth. Incorporate a high-quality, balanced feed enriched with protein to support the development of new feathers. Supplements like black oil sunflower seeds or mealworms can also aid in feather growth.

2. Hydration and Nutrition:

Ensure your chickens have access to fresh water. Hydration is crucial during molting. Supplement their diet with vitamins and minerals to support overall health and boost the molting process.

3. Environmental Considerations:

Provide a comfortable and secure environment for molting chickens. Maintain a clean coop, free from drafts, and offer additional bedding for warmth. Consider using a red heat lamp to provide gentle warmth without disrupting their natural light-dark cycle.

4. Minimize Stress:

Reduce stressors during molting by minimizing disturbances. Avoid unnecessary handling or movements that could lead to additional feather loss. Implement gradual changes in the environment to prevent sudden disruptions.

Coping with Egg Laying Issues: Enhancing Productivity

1. Nutrient-Rich Diet:

Ensure your chickens receive a nutritionally balanced diet that supports egg production. A diet rich in calcium and protein promotes strong eggshells and overall reproductive health. Consider layer feed or supplements to meet these specific nutritional requirements.

2. Adequate Nesting Spaces:

Provide suitable nesting boxes that are clean, comfortable, and secluded. Chickens prefer privacy when laying eggs, so ensure nesting boxes are well-protected and situated away from high-traffic areas. Maintain a ratio of one nesting box per three to four hens.

3. Stress Reduction:

Minimize stressors in the coop by addressing overcrowding, aggressive behavior, or environmental changes. A calm and stress-free environment promotes consistent egg production. Consider introducing environmental enrichment such as perches or toys to reduce boredom.

4. Regular Egg Collection:

Collect eggs promptly and regularly to prevent broodiness, egg-eating, or other undesirable behaviors. Inspect eggs for soft shells, blood spots, or irregularities. Prompt collection also helps maintain cleanliness in the nesting boxes.

5. Light Management:

Control lighting conditions to mimic natural daylight cycles. Adequate light exposure encourages regular egg laying. Supplemental lighting in the coop during winter can help sustain egg production.

<u>**Monitoring and Adjusting Strategies:**</u>

<u>**Continuous Improvement**</u>

1. Regular Health Checks:

Conduct regular health assessments to ensure your chickens are in optimal condition. Address any signs of illness, discomfort, or abnormalities promptly.

2. Observation and Record-Keeping:

Keep detailed records of molting and egg-laying patterns. Note any deviations or concerns, and adjust your strategies accordingly. Consistent observation allows for proactive management.

3. Consulting Professionals:

Seek advice from poultry veterinarians or experienced poultry keepers if challenges persist. Professionals can provide tailored solutions based on your flock's specific needs and conditions.

By implementing these comprehensive strategies, you can successfully cope with molting and egg-laying issues, promoting the health and productivity of your chicken flock.

Comprehensive Strategies for Identifying and Addressing Common Ailments and Injuries in Chickens

Effectively recognizing and treating common illnesses and injuries in chickens is pivotal for ensuring the overall well-being of your flock. These health challenges, stemming from various factors like pathogens, accidents, or environmental conditions, demand a meticulous approach for accurate diagnosis and targeted treatment. Here's a comprehensive guide to help you navigate the complexities of managing chicken health:

<u>Recognizing Illnesses and Injuries: A Systematic Approach</u>

1. Observation Skills:

Develop keen observation skills to detect subtle changes in your chickens' behavior, appearance, or daily routines. Pay attention to indicators like lethargy, reduced appetite, abnormal posture, or changes in droppings.

2. Physical Examination:

Conduct routine physical examinations to identify external signs of illnesses or injuries. Inspect your chickens' eyes, ears, beak, comb, wattles, feathers, legs, and vent for abnormalities, wounds, or swelling.

3. Behavioral Observations:

Monitor social interactions within the flock. Aggressive behavior, isolation, or changes in the pecking order can indicate underlying issues. Note any abnormal vocalizations or withdrawal from usual activities.

4. Diagnostic Resources:

Utilize reliable resources such as poultry health guides, reputable websites, or professional veterinary advice. Familiarize yourself with common chicken diseases, symptoms, and diagnostic tools to enhance your diagnostic capabilities.

<u>Treating Illnesses and Injuries: Targeted and Safe Interventions</u>

1. Medication and Vaccination:

Administer appropriate medications or vaccines based on the diagnosed illness. Consult with a veterinarian to determine the correct dosage and administration method. Vaccination schedules can help prevent certain diseases.

2. Isolation:

Separate affected chickens from the flock to prevent the spread of contagious illnesses. Create a designated quarantine area with proper ventilation, warmth, and access to food and water.

3. Hygiene and Cleaning:

Maintain a clean and hygienic coop environment to reduce the risk of infections. Regularly clean bedding, nesting boxes, and feeding areas. Remove feces promptly to minimize the presence of harmful bacteria.

4. Wound Care and Bandaging:

Attend to injuries promptly by cleaning wounds with a mild antiseptic solution. Use bandages or wound dressings to protect injuries from dirt and pecking. Monitor healing progress and seek professional advice if needed.

5. Surgical Interventions:

In severe cases, surgical procedures may be required. Seek professional veterinary guidance for surgeries like wound suturing, abscess drainage, or other necessary interventions.

6. Supportive Care:

Provide extra care and attention to ailing chickens. Ensure they can access fresh water, palatable food, and a comfortable environment. Supplement their diet with nutrients that support recovery.

Monitoring and Prevention: Proactive Health Management

1. Regular Checkups:

Schedule routine health checkups for your flock. Regular veterinary inspections can help detect potential issues before they escalate.

2. Biosecurity Measures:

Implement biosecurity measures to prevent the introduction of pathogens. Control visitor access, practice proper sanitation, and avoid contact with other poultry flocks.

3. Record Keeping:

Maintain detailed records of health observations, treatments, and vaccinations. A comprehensive record-keeping system aids in tracking health trends and facilitating timely interventions.

4. Environmental Management:

Optimize the coop environment by providing adequate ventilation, lighting, and space. Minimize stressors such as overcrowding, temperature extremes, or exposure to drafts.

By adhering to these comprehensive strategies, you empower yourself to identify, treat, and prevent common illnesses and injuries in your chicken flock, fostering a healthier and more resilient poultry community.

Conclusion

As we part ways on this exhilarating journey into chicken keeping, I invite you to bask in the newfound knowledge, the enchanting tales of breeds, and the empowering wisdom that now rests in your hands. Your venture into coops, clucks, and caretaking has just begun.

Picture the mornings filled with the symphony of contented clucks, the aroma of fresh straw in your coop, and the joy of gathering eggs warm from the nesting box. This isn't just a guide; it's an invitation to a lifestyle enriched by the feathers and personalities of your feathered companions.

But, our journey doesn't end here. It takes **flight** into the vast expanse of possibilities that

chicken keeping unfolds. As you embark on your chicken-raising odyssey, remember to **embrace** the unpredictable, revel in the simple joys, and let the unique quirks of each feathered friend become a cherished chapter in your story.

Your experience is a tapestry woven with threads of dedication, passion, and a profound understanding of the delicate dance between caretaker and chicken. Cherish every crow of the rooster, every dust bath taken, and every egg collected – for these moments, my fellow poultry enthusiast, are the heartbeats of your journey.

Now, I implore you, dear reader, to take a moment and reflect. Let the echoes of your "why" resonate within you. Why did you embark on this adventure? Was it the promise of fresh eggs, the allure of heritage breeds, or the simple joy of connecting with nature? Whatever it may be, hold onto that flame. Nurture it, let it blaze, and guide your every stride in the enchanting dance of chicken keeping.

As you turn the last page of this book, I invite you to leave a trail of your footsteps in the soil of your poultry haven. Dive into the richness of the experience, savor the challenges, celebrate the victories, and, above all, share your story.

Your review is not just a testament to these pages; it's a beacon to fellow enthusiasts, beckoning them to join the ranks of those who have discovered the profound joy of raising chickens.

Practice your newfound knowledge with love, patience, and the dedication that sparked your journey. Your coop is not merely a shelter for chickens; it's a sanctuary for dreams, aspirations, and the unique bond that grows between a keeper and their flock.

Now, with a heart brimming with enthusiasm and a mind teeming with possibilities, go forth and create your poultry masterpiece. Your chickens await, and so does a vibrant community of like-minded individuals. Share, learn, and continue to be inspired.

Remember, this is not farewell. It's a **"cluck you later,"** as your journey with chickens unfolds. Thank you for entrusting me with a part of your adventure. May your coop be ever-bustling, your eggs plentiful, and your connection with these feathered friends everlasting.

In gratitude,
[Unique Kade]

Bonus

<u>Ten Delicious Recipes for You</u>

1. Egg Drop Soup

Introduction:

Egg Drop Soup is a simple and delicious soup with eggs as the main ingredient.

Ingredients:

- 4 cups of water or chicken broth
- 4 eggs
- Salt and pepper, to taste
- 2 teaspoons of soy sauce (optional)
- 2 tablespoons of green onions, chopped (optional)
- 1 tablespoon of cornstarch dissolved in 2 tablespoons of water (optional)

Mode of Preparation:

- In a small bowl, beat the eggs with a fork or a whisk until well blended. Set aside.

- Bring the water or broth to a boil over high heat in a large pot. Reduce the heat to medium-high and keep it at a gentle boil.

- Slowly pour the beaten eggs into the pot, stirring gently with a fork or a whisk in one direction. The eggs will form thin strands or soft curds as they cook in the hot liquid.

- Add the salt, pepper, soy sauce, and green onions and combine. If you want a thicker soup, add the cornstarch mixture and stir until the soup is slightly thickened.

- Turn off the heat and ladle the soup into bowls. Enjoy it while it's hot.

Why the Recipe Works:

- It works because it is very nutritious and satisfying, providing protein, hydration, and warmth from the eggs and the liquid. It also provides vitamins and minerals from the green onions, soy sauce, and cornstarch.

2. Chicken and Mushroom Pie

Introduction:

It's perfect for a cozy dinner or a special occasion.

Ingredients:

★ 2 cups of cooked chicken, shredded or chopped

★ 2 cups of mushrooms, sliced

★ 1 can of cream of chicken soup

★ 1/4 cup of milk

★ 2 tablespoons of butter

★ 2 tablespoons of flour

★ Salt and pepper, to taste

★ A pinch of nutmeg

★ 1 package of refrigerated pie crust or homemade pie crust

Mode of Preparation:

★ Preheat the oven to 375°F and lightly grease a 9-inch pie dish.

★ In a large skillet over medium-high heat, melt the butter and cook the mushrooms for about 15 minutes, stirring occasionally, until browned and tender.

★ Sprinkle the flour over the mushrooms and stir to combine. Cook for another 2 minutes, stirring constantly, until the flour is cooked.

★ Add the cream of chicken soup, milk, salt, pepper, and nutmeg, and stir to combine. Bring the mixture to a boil, then reduce the heat and simmer for about 10 minutes, stirring occasionally, until slightly thickened.

★ Stir in the chicken and remove from the heat.

★ Unroll one pie crust and fit it into the prepared pie dish, trimming and crimping the edges. Spoon the chicken and mushroom mixture over the crust, spreading it evenly.

★ Unroll the other pie crust and place it over the filling, tucking and crimping the edges. Cut some slits on the top crust to vent the steam.

★ Bake the pie for about 25 minutes until the crust is golden and the filling is bubbly.

★ Let the pie rest for 10 minutes before slicing and serving.

Why the Recipe Works:

★ It works because it is versatile and customizable, as you can use any cooked chicken you have, such as leftovers from another meal, rotisserie, or canned. You can also use mushrooms like white, cremini, or portobello. You can add some cheese, herbs, or spices to the filling.

3. Chicken Pot Pie

Introduction:

It's a great way to use any leftover vegetables in your fridge or pantry.

Ingredients:

- 2 cups of cooked chicken, shredded or chopped
- 2 cups of mixed vegetables, such as carrots, peas, corn, etc.
- 1 can of cream of mushroom soup, or any other soup you like
- 1/4 cup of milk, or half-and-half
- 2 tablespoons of butter or margarine
- 2 tablespoons of flour or cornstarch
- Salt and pepper, to taste

- A pinch of nutmeg, optional

- 1 package of refrigerated pie crust or homemade pie crust

Mode of Preparation:

- Preheat the oven to 375°F and lightly grease a 9-inch pie dish.

- In a small saucepan over medium heat, melt the butter and whisk in the flour, salt, pepper, and nutmeg. Cook for about 2 minutes, stirring constantly, until the mixture is smooth and bubbly.

- Gradually whisk in the soup and milk and bring the mixture to a boil. Reduce the heat and simmer for about 10 minutes, stirring occasionally, until slightly thickened.

- Stir in the chicken and vegetables and remove from the heat.

- Unroll one pie crust and fit it into the prepared pie dish, trimming and crimping the edges. Spoon the chicken and vegetable mixture over the crust, spreading it evenly.

- Unroll the other pie crust and place it over the filling, tucking and crimping the edges. Cut some slits on the top crust to vent the steam.

- Bake the pie for about 25 minutes until the crust is golden and the filling is bubbly.

- Let the pie rest for 10 minutes before slicing and serving.

Why the Recipe Works:

- It works because it is versatile and customizable, as you can use any cooked chicken you have, such as leftovers from another meal, rotisserie, or canned. You can also use any vegetables or soup you like.

4. Egg Salad Croissants

Introduction:

Egg Salad Croissants are flaky and buttery croissants. They are ideal for breakfast or brunch on weekends or holidays.

Ingredients:

★ 6 hard-boiled eggs, peeled and chopped

★ 1/4 cup of mayonnaise, or yogurt

★ 2 teaspoons of mustard or relish

★ 1/4 cup of celery, sliced thin

★ 2 tablespoons of onion, sliced thin

★ Salt and pepper, to taste

★ 4 croissants, preferably large

★ **Optional:** lettuce, tomato, cheese, or any other toppings you like

Mode of Preparation:

★ Combine the eggs, mayonnaise, mustard, celery, onion, salt, and pepper in a large bowl. Mix well until everything is well coated and combined.

★ Preheat the oven to 375°F and line a baking sheet with parchment paper or cooking spray.

★ Cut the croissants in half horizontally, place them on the prepared baking sheet, and cut side up. Bake for 10 minutes or until the croissants are lightly toasted and warm.

★ Spoon about 1/4 cup of the egg salad mixture onto the bottom half of each croissant. Top with other toppings you like, such as lettuce, tomato, cheese, etc. Cover with the top half of the croissants and press lightly to seal.

★ Enjoy while warm or at room temperature.

Why the Recipe Works:

★ It works because it is very nutritious and satisfying, providing protein, fiber, and healthy fats, from eggs, mayonnaise, and croissants. It also provides vitamins and minerals from the celery, onion, lettuce, tomato, and cheese.

5. Chicken Fried Rice:

Introduction:

Chicken Fried Rice offers a quick and effortless culinary solution; this dish is ideal for repurposing leftovers, which cater to both convenience and flavor, making it a perfect choice for hosting gatherings or serving a delightful family dinner.

Ingredients:

- 4 cups cold or day-old cooked rice
- 2 cups cooked, bite-sized chicken pieces

- 4 green onions, sliced (white and green parts separated)
- 2 cloves minced garlic
- 1 tsp grated ginger
- 1/4 cup soy sauce
- 2 tbsp sesame oil
- 1/4 tsp red pepper flakes
- Salt and pepper to taste
- 2 tsp sesame seeds
- 1 cup thawed frozen green peas
- 1/2 cup shredded carrots
- 1/2 cup corn kernels (fresh or frozen)
- 1/4 cup sliced water chestnuts, drained
- 1/4 cup cooked, shelled edamame beans
- 2 tbsp chopped scallions for garnish

Mode of Preparation:

- Stir-fry white parts of green onions, garlic, ginger, and red pepper flakes in 1 tbsp sesame oil until fragrant.

- Add chicken and soy sauce, stir-frying until coated. Set aside.

- Stir-fry rice in remaining sesame oil until hot and slightly crisp.

- Add green parts of green onions, sesame seeds, peas, carrots, corn, water chestnuts, and edamame beans. Stir-fry until vegetables are tender.

- Season with salt and pepper, garnish with scallions.

- Serve hot, optionally, with more soy sauce.

Why the Recipe Works:

- This recipe works due to its simplicity, quick preparation (around 30 minutes), and accessibility without requiring special skills or equipment.

- Nutritionally balanced, it provides protein, carbs, fiber, and vitamins, offering a wholesome and satisfying meal.

6. Egg and Cheese Quesadillas:

Introduction:

Egg and Cheese Quesadillas are a delightful combination of cheesy and crispy. These quesadillas are perfect for a quick weekend breakfast or brunch.

Ingredients:

★ 4 eggs

★ 1/4 cup milk

★ Salt and pepper to taste

★ 2 tbsp butter

★ 8 flour tortillas

★ 2 cups shredded cheese

★ 1/2 cup salsa

★ 1/4 cup sour cream (optional)

★ Optional toppings: cilantro, jalapeños

Mode of Preparation:

★ Whisk eggs with milk, salt, and pepper.

★ Cook egg mixture in butter until scrambled; set aside.

★ Fill tortillas with cheese, eggs, and salsa; cook until golden and crisp.

★ Optional: Add toppings like cilantro or jalapeños.

★ Cut into wedges and serve with optional sour cream.

Why the Recipe Works:

★ This recipe's simplicity, quick preparation (around 20 minutes), and minimal requirements make it accessible.

7. Chicken and Egg Salad Sandwiches:

Introduction:

These sandwiches are versatile and convenient for a quick lunch or snack, suitable for picnics, potlucks, or make-ahead meals.

Ingredients:

- 2 cups cooked, shredded chicken
- 4 hard-boiled eggs, chopped
- 1/4 cup mayonnaise
- 1/4 cup diced celery
- 2 tbsp minced onion
- Salt and pepper to taste
- 8 slices of bread or lettuce leaves
- Optional toppings: lettuce, tomato, cheese

Mode of Preparation:

- Mix chicken, eggs, mayonnaise, celery, onion, salt, and pepper.

- Spoon onto bread or lettuce; add optional toppings.

- Assemble sandwiches and enjoy. Store in the fridge if needed.

Why the Recipe Works:

The recipe's simplicity (around 15 minutes), common ingredients, and adaptability make it accessible.

8. Egg and Cheese Quesadillas

Introduction:

Egg and Cheese Quesadillas are cheesy and crispy quesadillas. It is ideal for breakfast or brunch on weekends or holidays.

Ingredients:

- ★ 4 eggs
- ★ 1/4 cup of milk
- ★ Salt and pepper, to taste
- ★ 2 tablespoons of butter

★ 8 tortillas, preferably flour

★ 2 cups of shredded cheese, any kind

★ 1/2 cup of salsa, any kind

★ 1/4 cup of sour cream, optional

★ **Optional:** cilantro, jalapeños, or any other toppings you like

Mode of Preparation:

★ Whisk the eggs with the milk, salt, and pepper in a small bowl until well blended. Set aside.

★ In a large skillet over medium-high heat, melt the butter and cook the egg mixture, stirring occasionally, until the eggs are set and scrambled, about 10 minutes.

★ Transfer the eggs to a plate and keep warm.

★ Wipe the skillet clean and return it to the heat. Place one tortilla on the skillet and evenly sprinkle 1/4 cup of cheese over it.

Spoon 1/4 of the eggs over the cheese, and spread 2 tablespoons of salsa over the eggs. Top with another tortilla and press lightly to seal.

★ Cook for about 3 minutes per side or until the cheese is melted and the tortillas are golden and crisp. Repeat with the remaining tortillas, cheese, eggs, and salsa to make 4 quesadillas.

★ Cut the quesadillas into wedges and serve with sour cream, if desired, and any other toppings you like.

Why the Recipe Works:

This recipe works because it is very simple and easy to make, as it only takes about 20 minutes from start to finish and does not require any special equipment or skills.

9. Lemon Herb Grilled Chicken Skewers

Introduction:

These skewers have a delightful blend of citrusy brightness and savory herbs, ideal for a barbecue, creating a mouthwatering experience for any outdoor gathering or family dinner.

Ingredients:

- 2 lbs boneless, skinless chicken breasts cut into bite-sized cubes
- Zest and juice of 2 lemons
- 3 tbsp olive oil
- 3 cloves garlic, minced
- 2 tsp dried oregano
- 2 tsp dried thyme
- 1 tsp paprika
- Salt and black pepper to taste
- Wooden skewers soaked in water

Mode of Preparation:

- Mix lemon zest, lemon juice, olive oil, minced garlic, oregano, thyme, paprika, salt, and black pepper to create the marinade.

- Add chicken cubes to the marinade, ensuring an even coating. Refrigerate for at least 30 minutes to let the flavors infuse.
- Preheat the grill to medium-high heat.
- Thread marinated chicken cubes onto soaked wooden skewers, leaving a small space between each piece.
- Grill skewers for 10-12 minutes, turning occasionally, until chicken is cooked and has a nice char.
- Garnish with fresh herbs or additional lemon zest if desired.
- Serve hot with grilled vegetables, rice, or a refreshing salad.

Why the Recipe Works:

- This recipe introduces a refreshing twist to grilled chicken, combining the brightness of lemon with aromatic herbs for a unique and vibrant flavor profile.

10. Honey Garlic Baked Chicken Thighs

Introduction:

Honey Garlic Baked Chicken Thighs are a delectable combination of sweet and savory, creating a sticky and flavorful glaze over tender, oven-baked chicken thighs. This easy-to-make dish offers a perfect balance of honey sweetness, garlic richness, and a hint of soy sauce for depth. Ideal for a hassle-free weeknight dinner or a family feast, these chicken thighs are sure to become a favorite.

Ingredients:

- ★ 8 bone-in, skin-on chicken thighs
- ★ 1/4 cup honey

★ 3 tbsp soy sauce

★ 4 cloves garlic, minced

★ 2 tbsp olive oil

★ 1 tsp dried thyme

★ 1/2 tsp smoked paprika

★ Salt and black pepper to taste

★ Fresh parsley, chopped, for garnish

Mode of Preparation:

★ Preheat the oven to 400°F (200°C). Line a baking dish with parchment paper or lightly grease it.

★ Whisk together honey, soy sauce, minced garlic, olive oil, dried thyme, smoked paprika, salt, and black pepper in a bowl.

★ Place the chicken thighs in the prepared baking dish.

★ Brush each chicken thigh generously with the honey-garlic mixture, ensuring an even coating.

★ Bake in the oven for 30-35 minutes or until the chicken reaches an internal temperature of 165°F (74°C) and has a golden-brown glaze.

★ Remove the chicken from the oven and let it rest for a few minutes.

★ Garnish with chopped fresh parsley before serving.

★ Serve the Honey Garlic Baked Chicken Thighs with your favorite sides, such as roasted vegetables, mashed potatoes, or a crisp salad.

Why the Recipe Works:

Using bone-in, skin-on chicken thighs ensures juicy and flavorful meat, while the skin crisps up during baking for added texture.

Honey Garlic Baked Chicken Thighs offer a versatile main dish that pairs well with various sides, making it a versatile option for any occasion.

Thank you for reading Clucks to Chicken

In gratitude,

[Unique Kade]